“This isn’t just a book; it’s a spiritual devot
heart, turn you back toward God, and hel
times painful but also liberating season of ... empty
nest. Though there is much wise and practical advice, in the end Michele offers hope and turns us back to dependence upon God. I was challenged, encouraged, and renewed to make these empty-nest years ones filled with joy instead of worry; hope instead of despair; and new promise instead of old regret.”

—Gary Thomas
Author of *Sacred Marriage* and *A Lifelong Love*

“In her new book *Empty Nest, What’s Next?* Michele Howe captures perfectly the angst and challenges associated with being an empty nester and a parent of adult children. She hits all the important topics we never think about, and lays them out in a concise and easy-to-read manner.”

—Rick Johnson
Best-selling author of *Becoming Your Spouse’s Better Half*, *That’s My Son*, and *That’s My Teenage Son*

“I am an empty nester so I know—no, *I guarantee*: If you are a parent, you will *need* this book at some point in your life. Empty nesting is a difficult time of life and Michele Howe’s words are the bandage you will need to help heal, whether you require a companion during a good cry or a wise counselor to point the way ahead. I wish I’d had Michele’s book when I was limping through the empty-nest stage.”

—Jeannie St. John Taylor
Author, illustrator, radio host

“Michele Howe’s *Empty Nest* is chock-full of stories, wisdom, candor, and comfort. Her conversational and transparent style is like sitting across the table with a dear friend. As an empty-nest mom I can relate to the rich content in each chapter. What a terrific book this would be for a women’s book study.”

—Brenda Nixon
Author, *Beyond Buggies and Bonnets: Seven True Stories of Former Amish*
Speaker and award-winning blogger at www.BrendaNixonOnAmish.blogspot.com

"In Michele Howe's new book she covers every significant aspect of the sometimes-beautiful/sometimes-brutal journey of learning to be the parent of a grownup. 'It was only when I dropped to my knees before the Lord and pleaded with him to help me transfer ownership of my child to his care that I was able to let go.' Wow! I've been there. Her stories range from raw to sweet to fun, but they all contain deeply relatable truth. I saw myself in many, and I saw my mom and friends in others. The transition from mommy to peer, friend, and occasional counselor (by invitation only) is made a little easier with this book."

—Diane Markins
Speaker, trainer, radio host of *Bold Living*

"In *Empty Nest, What's Next?* author Michele Howe meets parents at the celebratory and confusing crossroad between nurturing lively offspring and relating to adult children. Joyfully we celebrate their wings, also suddenly aware that the children who once were the center of our focus now captain their own lives. Having launched my own seven grown children, I know parents must make the transition to establish a healthy peer-to-peer relationship. With gentleness and insight born of experience, *Empty Nest, What's Next?* tells you how. Thirty practical chapters address issues from meeting potential love interests to giving advice and helping through a crisis. Always at the center are faith, family, and unconditional love for our grown children."

—PeggySue Wells
Best-selling author of *The Slave across the Street*,
***Rediscovering Your Happily Ever After*,**
Für Elise*, and *Bonding with Your Child through Boundaries

"*Empty Nest, What's Next?* should be required reading for all parents of adult children. If you are struggling with how involved to be in the lives of your adult children, or if you are raising your grandchildren due to unexpected circumstances, you will find valuable encouragement, helpful advice, and biblical wisdom in this excellent book. I suggest reading the 30 chapters one at a time, over a 30-day time period. Follow through with the 'Take-away Action Thought' at the end of each chapter, and make the ending prayer your own heart-cry to God. This is a must-read book!"

—Carol Kent
Speaker and author of *Unquenchable: Grow a Wildfire Faith that Will Endure Anything*

Empty Nest, What's Next?

Parenting Adult Children Without Losing Your Mind

Empty Nest, What's Next?

Parenting Adult Children Without Losing Your Mind

MICHELE HOWE

Empty Nest, What's Next? Parenting Adult Children without Losing Your Mind

P. O. Box 3473
Peabody, Massachusetts 01961-3473

ISBN 978-1-61970-666-8

Printed in the United States of America

Second Printing—September 2018

Library of Congress Cataloging-in-Publication Data

Howe, Michele.
Empty nest, what's next? : parenting adult children without losing your mind / Michele Howe.
pages cm
ISBN 978-1-61970-666-8 (alk. paper)
1. Parent and adult child—Religious aspects—Christianity. 2. Parents—Religious life. 3. Empty nesters—Family relationships. 4. Adult children—Family relationships. I. Title.
BV4529.H697 2015
248.8'45—dc23
2015016676

To my two grandbabies who are thriving in the light of God's perfect love in heaven.

I can't wait to meet you both someday!

Contents

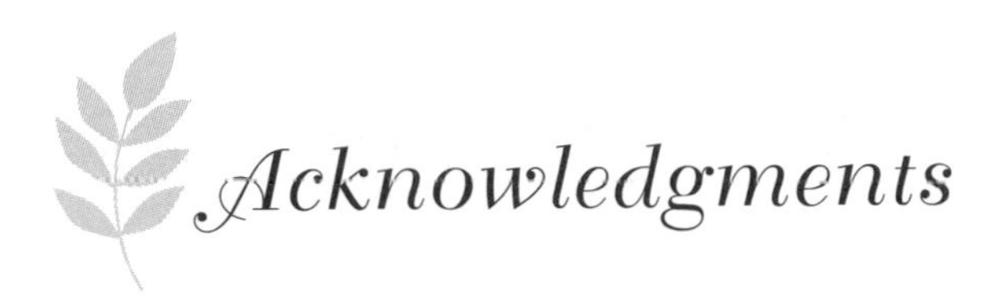

Acknowledgments

Between the time when the first page is written and a reader completes the final page, months upon months have passed, and hours upon hours have been invested in each and every book published. From the first notion of a new book's premise to the finely crafted final product, countless professionals offer their talents and giftedness to create a resource that will reach far and deep into the hearts of those who open its pages.

For every author, it is a humble privilege to accept a book contract from a publisher who believes in the author's message. For that honor, I want to thank Hendrickson's editorial director, Patricia Anders, for her enthusiasm, kindness, and support of this project. I am excited to see what God will do with this book as it reaches those parents who (like me) are in need of some encouragement and perspective in this zany (but exciting) empty-nest season of life.

For bringing their expertise to this work, I would also like to thank Tina Donohue for her design of this book, Phil Frank for typesetting it, and Meg Rusick for helping promote it.

And, finally, thanks to my longstanding agent, Les Stobbe, who has seen my highs and lows in this always-changing publishing industry and has kept me even-keeled through it all. Les, you are much appreciated.

Introduction

People always told me the most difficult parenting years were from birth to eighteen years of age. They were wrong. Not to be discouraging to younger parents, but with every year that passes your child inches his way out of your control, and eventually out of your home. Who knew how much emotional distress this never-ending transition could cause us parents?

Which is why and how *Empty Nest, What's Next? Parenting Adult Children without Losing Your Mind* came into being. The longer I parented my now adult children, the more I realized I was in over my head. I quickly recognized I needed some useful instruction, along with some daily encouragement that would help me keep an eternal perspective on all the going-on around me.

This book will help parents make the adjustment from full-time parenting to empty-nest parenting, and do it with grace and style. Since parenting is a role that is constantly growing and evolving in the same way that individual family members grow and evolve, there are specific challenges to parenting our adult children that are rarely addressed. *Empty Nest, What's Next?* will equip parents to enter into this dynamic season of life with the tools they need to navigate it successfully (from their perspective, as well as from their adult children's perspective). Oh, happy thought.

Along the way, we'll discover that God is right in the center of every challenge, every change. He's there to offer hope, guidance, and counsel when we really don't have a clue as to how to get to the other side of our children's adult problems. Best of all, we'll find some comic relief as we come to understand that we aren't alone in this journey, and that God will show us what it looks like to parent our kids even when they aren't "kids" anymore. Let's get started!

Chapter 1

Entering the Empty Nest (or Almost There)

Surely goodness and mercy shall follow me
all the days of my life:
and I will dwell in the house of the LORD
forever.

Psalm 23:6

We drop anchor in the goodness of God.
Paula Rinehart

I still remember how the Midwest fall's dampness chilled my bones and then crept right into my heart that dreary afternoon when we dropped my son off at college for the first time. I wept most of the way home, which certainly surprised me more than it did my husband, who stoically drove while patting me on the shoulder.

It's been five years now since that torrent of tears exploded from somewhere deep inside, again reminding me that my full-time season of mothering had come to an end. Curiously, handing my only son off to fend for himself in a nearby college town wasn't my first step toward reaching the empty nest. Two of his three older sisters had already moved out and married, but this desolate feeling was different. Completely different. As I contemplated why I was so upset about my son moving away, it hit me that I was grieving the death of a life I'd put everything into for over twenty-five years.

Swirling around in my heart and mind were memories of my four children's births, their childhoods, teen years, and now this—young adulthood. While I was thankful each of my children was growing up and out of the home, there was another part of me that felt unsettled and unanchored. Who was I now?

Could it be that I had become one of "those" mothers who hadn't prepared for the empty nest although they saw it coming full speed ahead for years previous? Not me. I was always looking to the coming months and years in happy anticipation, while simultaneously preparing for these major life changes. So then, what was wrong with me?

In one of my less emotional and more analytical moments, I realized it didn't matter how much I'd looked ahead and/or planned and prepared—the heart will still break all the same when someone you love leaves for good. Someone I loved had just left for good, and it hurt. I know life is always in motion—nothing ever remains the same, which isn't a bad thing. What I needed to embrace was a future that looked different but was full of new and as yet unattained promising experiences.

After shedding more tears than I counted as "normal," I started to wake up to the possibilities of my new season of life. Slowly I found I was able to wrap my heart and mind around that fact of my new empty nest in a glad way. Time passed and the tears were replaced by a God-given grace-upon-grace, a sure and certain genuine hopeful expectancy. My fulltime mothering might be history, but I certainly wasn't. Oh, happy thought.

One of the benefits of watching the seasons of life pass swiftly by is that we gain a more realistic perspective on life as a whole. The longer we live, the more we recognize how little of life is unchanging. Our bodies grow and mature. Our material possessions grow old and break down. Our cars and homes deteriorate and lose their worth over time. Truly, the only lasting values in life are people. Our relationships with our families, friends, neighbors, and colleagues are what bring the fullness to life—eternally. So when one season of life comes to a close (or, as in parenting, takes on a new direction), we would do well to first accept the change, and then embrace and gently enter into it. Slowly. Certainly. Always working toward this "new normal" with the grace God promises us.

True enough, there's a whole lot of shaking and shifting that goes on in the heart and mind of a mother who has spent the bulk of her adult years investing herself, her gifts, talents, and treasures into her children. But as every woman of faith knows, God never wastes pain, especially pain of the heart. He uses it to his glory and our good. May each of us, who has had the supreme privilege of raising children to adulthood, learn to step out of the spotlight of their lives when that time comes, and prayerfully support and applaud where God leads them. As we make this intentional choice to trust God for their futures as well as our own, we'll enjoy a front-row seat to some very remarkable happenings that can only be orchestrated and overseen by our great and gracious God.

Take-away Action Thought

When the foundation of my life shakes and shifts, only your love will anchor me safely through.

My Heart's Cry to You, O Lord

Lord, I am ever grateful that you understand what I'm feeling these days. Everything and everyone that surrounds me is changing and it scares me. Some moments I feel strong and courageous and ready for the next step. But often, I'm left wondering who I am now that my children are leaving my care. I feel pulled from every direction, into the past where I am comfortable, and into the future where I'm not sure it will lead. Help me, Lord, to take one day at a time, fully confident that you will safely direct me, sustain me, and lead me with your goodness and mercy. Amen.

Chapter 2

Accepting that Parenting Mistakes Are Done Deals

To you they cried out and were saved;
in you they trusted and were not put to shame.
Psalm 22:5

We come into the world needy, and
we leave it the same way.
Randy Alcorn

Make up the difference. Make up the difference. Make up the difference. If I'd whispered that phrase once to the Lord, I'd repeated it over one thousand times as I parented my children while they were still under our roof. Now, with three gone and one on her way out, I'm still saying it—maybe even more now than then.

I'd be lying if I said I didn't feel some measure of neediness every single day all along my parenting journey. Sure, some days, maybe even weeks, I'd feel more comfortable, more confident that my husband and I were on the right track with our parenting. But what I recall most vividly were the times when I was on my knees before the Lord begging him to help us understand one of our children better, help us to know how to love them more powerfully, help us to communicate how much we cared even when we disciplined them.

If you're seeing a repetitive pattern here of asking for help, you have a pretty accurate picture of how we parented our children from the time they were infants to the present day. I believe I always knew I didn't have enough wisdom, grace, and even love (the unconditional kind) that would be required day in and day out to be the mother my children (all children) need—which is why I latched on to that single phrase of "Make up the difference" as soon as I heard another parent say it.

Something about the desperation of the plea resonated deeply within my mother's heart because I knew. I recognized full well that I couldn't do this parenting job in my own strength. Still, as much aware as I was (and still am) that in my own strength my children wouldn't receive all they required to grow into the adults God desired them to become, I failed. A lot.

Looking back, I still recall specific parenting moments that bring a stab of pain and sorrow to me because of the harsh words I spoke (and then quickly regretted); the lack of patience I demonstrated when my children came to me brimming over with excitement and wanting to share with me (but I was too busy or preoccupied to notice); and how I frequently found myself wishing away whatever season of life we were in because I wrongly believed the next season would be easier (for me).

Ironically, even these regret-ridden memories have taught me a few things. Of all the past failings I've experienced, I've learned a lot too. I'm confident that God heard the prayers of an ill-equipped young mother (now a middle-aged mother) and that he did "make up the difference."

Yes, he did—even when I failed not once, not twice, but countless times. God was good and gracious and forgave me, and then he picked me up off the floor in defeat and gave me the strength to go to my children and try again. *Make up the difference.* Isn't that a beautiful statement? I've grown to love it more and more as I've watched our faithful God prove how trustworthy he is when we come all dirty and dusty and undone.

No matter what our age, we are needy people. We are born needy, we live needy, and we die needy. Jesus knows this about us. So it is a wonder that God chose the family unit as the primary place, the safe haven, for the majority of growing and maturity to take place. God isn't surprised by our parental failings. He isn't sitting on the throne in heaven wringing his hands in despair when we blunder.

What God wants is for us to trust him—trust him enough to guide us, teach us, and lead us as we guide, teach, and lead our children. When we cry out to God in confusion and pain, he is faithful to answer us, to equip us, and to truly work in ways we can't imagine in our moments of discouragement and despair.

From the second our child is born to the final act of parental love toward that child, God is always working on our behalf to make up the difference. We should not be afraid that our failings, be they large or small, will be the undoing of our children. Instead, God would have us ask for forgiveness from those we've hurt, make reparations as needed, and then step forward in new and more loving ways. *Make up the difference.* Have you asked him to do that for you today?

Take-away Action Thought

Whenever I feel ill equipped to handle a parenting responsibility, I will call out to you, saying, "Make up the difference." And you will.

My Heart's Cry to You, O Lord

Lord, you know how sorrowful my heart is when I remember the times I failed to love my children in a way that honors you. It breaks my heart when I recall my words and some of my actions that were so angry, so selfish. It grieves me even now. Help me to learn from my mistakes, ask for forgiveness, and move forward. Only you can enable me to live in the now without being carried away with past regrets. Help me to trust you so much that I rest in confidence that you always have, and always will, make up the difference in me and in my children. Amen.

Chapter 3

Keeping First Things First–Faith Then Family

When hard pressed, I cried to the LORD;
he brought me into a spacious place.
Psalm 118:5

Freedom is an inside job.
Anonymous

For the better part of the last six years, I've been leading a small group where we read and discuss (and dismantle) one book after another. This is no lightweight women's book club where we chat, nibble on snacks, and promise to actually read the assigned chapters before the next meeting. Rather, we painstakingly read, highlight, and work through each sentence, each paragraph, and each page to thoroughly understand and digest the contents of every book we've selected to study. I love it.

The best part of these studies is the application of content to life, when at any moment you can look around the room and see the spark that lights up a woman's face as she realizes what she is reading can actually change her life (and set her free) for good. I've seen it happen more times than I can count, and it always thrills me when we "get it" that there is truth and application found in Scripture. But without the combination of both of those elements, not a whole lot changes. Truth plus application—that's where the real win happens. In a life. In a marriage. In a broken heart. In a wounded soul. Everywhere and all the time. That's where real freedom happens.

Whenever you gather women together to talk and discuss (and wrestle over truths), it is always an exciting prospect. It reminds me of the power of fellowshipping with those who are like-minded not just on reading choices, but on faith issues building our strong faith foundation more and more as the years pass. Just as we diligently put our energy into growing in our faith and placing it first in our lives, we become naturally more equipped to handle all of life's hardships. It's true that as we grow older we have to face numerous daily changes, challenges, and the consequences of our many accumulated choices. This in itself is daunting enough. But without a strong faith base on which to build a foundation for making decisions, facing tough times, and dealing rightly with consequences, we would be in over our heads.

Thus we need to continually invest in (and bolster up) our faith with our minds, hearts, and acts of our will. We alone decide where to place our energies, and if we aren't positioning ourselves to grow in intimacy with Christ daily on our own, and in the company of other Christians by learning and serving in a local church, we set ourselves up for eventual failure (if not tragedy) when hard times hit. And they will.

Only when we keep our faith first are we able to truly love and serve our growing family's needs as they grow and change and face their own challenges. Faith first. Family second. Freedom comes with applying that truth day by day.

Doubtless the message isn't a new one. We've all heard it said many times. But the truth is the truth is the truth. God's word instructs us to love him with all our minds, hearts, and souls. But do we? When was the last time we sat ourselves down and dug deeply into his powerful, life-giving book? How many times can you recall actually looking up a referenced Bible verse to find out what an unfamiliar word or phrase means? And what about putting into action the words you're reading? As my pastor is fond of reminding us, "Truth doesn't mean a thing until it's applied. Applied truth changes lives." Amen.

Before we sit back and rest easy on past biblical studies and feel too complacent, we need to remember that when our children come to us with a crisis situation, they don't need our opinions—they need biblical counsel direct from God's word. Only the truth as gleaned from the Bible will be robust enough to help them in their time of need and to set them free. Free from the inside-out type of freedom.

One other basic truth about putting God and his word first is that the truth gives freedom. Not the wimpy sort—the deep-down-into-the-heart-of-the-most-wounded-soul kind of freedom. And just like that old quote says, "Freedom is an inside job." It can't be bought or borrowed or begged. But it is free for the asking.

Take-away Action Thought

When my children come to me with a serious problem, I will not give them a simple solution until I've spent time searching for your wisdom in the Bible and praying.

My Heart's Cry to You, O Lord

Father, thank you for supplying us with everything we need to make wise and godly choices all through our lives. Help us to take the time to search out these truths daily, so that we are truly equipped to offer godly counsel to our children in their times of need. Remind us that worldly wisdom will never be enough and that it often shackles those in pain rather than release them. Keep us close to you through daily study, intentional prayer, and consistent fellowship with other believers in our local church. Help us to always put our faith first so that we can serve our family best. Amen.

Chapter 4

Learning to Step Back and Occasionally Advise

A thousand may fall at your side,
ten thousand at your right hand,
but it will not come near you.
Psalm 91:7

Life is a gift, albeit unassembled. It comes in pieces, and sometimes it falls to pieces. Part A doesn't always fit with part B. The struggle is too great for the strength. Inevitably, something seems to be missing. The pieces of life don't fit. When they don't, take your problem to Jesus.
Max Lucado

I plunked myself down in the booth of a well-known, well-worn breakfast eatery with a whole lot more on my mind than food and a steaming cup of coffee. On this particular fall morning, a last-minute breakfast date with a friend I'd known and loved for over four decades miraculously came together.

As often happens with friends who don't do so well at staying in touch in person but do far better at e-mailing and texting, once we met in person, we talked nonstop for almost four hours! Of course, with four adult children each and a couple of grandchildren and spouses to talk about, my friend and I did pretty well covering all our familial bases. But one statement hit me harder than any other—and that's saying a lot considering all the words exchanged between us.

We were on the topic of figuring out how to gracefully tackle tricky topics with our adult children, when we were dying to put our two cents in and just tell them what to do. My friend, wise woman that she is, looked at me and said we both needed to remember that when it comes right down to it, there's probably very little that parents need to say once their children grow up. After all, they've lived with us for at least the first eighteen years of their lives; listened to us teach them everything we deemed important; and they've watched us handle the good, the bad, and the ugly in life. In short, they've absorbed "us" into "them."

My friend continued gaining steam and passion as she spoke: *Pretty much I think our job now is to just listen, and only give advice when asked*. She's right.

Often most of my current frustration (as it relates to parenting) comes from me wanting to intervene, save the day, and rescue my children from what I imagine is certain disaster. More to the truth of the matter, what my children need most as young adults are parents who are at peace, who exude calmness, and are prepared to give them all their time and attention when it's requested. The bigger question is this: Am I willing to step aside, trust God, and allow my children to do some stumbling and falling along the way? To be honest, the only way that can happen is through God's grace at work inside of me. Every day, all day. No ifs, ands, or buts about it.

As parents, we raise our children to become independent, fully functioning, contributing members of society, don't we? Why then do so many parents short-circuit the maturation process by needlessly intervening when young adult children would benefit from all the wrestling and thinking through of making some of life's tough decisions? The answer is in one word: Fear.

I especially seem to out-distance my husband on this one. Because I tend to care so much and feel more, I am sadly prone to running too much interference for too long. Thus, because I'm not long-sighted enough (or are overrun by my own fears), I allow the what-ifs in life to unintentionally cause setbacks to growth in maturity in my children.

The only way mothers can truly step back into the advisory role of parenting is to steep themselves in the word of God by memorizing, meditating, and mulling over all the many promises in Scripture that combat fearful thinking and fear-based parenting. Letting our children go to make their own choices (and mistakes) is a good thing. It truly is.

Take-away Action Thought

The next time my children are getting ready to make a decision I may not fully agree with, I will pray before I speak. I will.

My Heart's Cry to You, O Lord

There is so much about letting go of my children that makes me feel afraid. I allow my imagination far too much space in my thinking, and I reflect back on my own mistakes in unhelpful ways that only increase my worries. Help me to learn from what I've done wrong in the past, and to use those experiences as fuel to pray more powerfully for my children as they face life and all of its crossroads. Jesus, you love my children more than I ever will, so by faith I give them and their choices to you. Please infuse your Holy Spirit-guided thoughts into every decision they make, and bless them for each one they make in obedience to you. When they don't obey you, Lord, then I relinquish them to you once again to steer them back to you in your way and in your time. Amen.

Chapter 5

Riding the Emotional Roller Coaster

You . . . have set my feet in a spacious place.
Psalm 31:8

We need to fight coolness with every fiber of our being. I want to stop admiring the cool, the detached people. I want to hug the messy, conflicted, honest, passionate people who are living their lives with enthusiasm.
Debbie Macomber

I'm convinced that one of the most telling ways to figure out what's going on in your life is to take a good look at your meal planning routine. It took me quite a while to get it through my brain that I didn't really need as much food on our dinner table each evening after our children moved out. At first, it felt strange paring back or halving every recipe. Unnatural even.

Finally, I got used to the fact that our children weren't dropping in to eat, staying for supper, or surprising us with a bunch of unexpected hungry friends. Even this small adjustment made my heart sting at times. Like lots of women, I love to cook and feed those I care about. The kitchen, be it large or small, is the natural gathering place in most homes. I sincerely believe it's the fragrant smells, the sight of something delicious simmering on the stove, and the small talk that goes on while the meal is being prepared that just draws folks to this center place and keeps them there long after the meal has been consumed.

So when the happy and full kitchen becomes rather quiet and lonely, emotions can take similar directions. While I am not complaining about having to cook less (in amounts or frequency), I now understand how these days being more subdued, slower-paced, and definitely quieter, can trigger some emotional sadness. During those hours of the day that used to be frantic with food prep, laundry, playing chauffer, teacher, doctor, counselor, and more, I find the quietness of moment somewhat unsettling. Or at least I did.

After listening to myself talk to myself about feeling low and out of sorts one silent afternoon, I started listening in earnest to a speaker who shared about living in the moment. We've all heard these pick-me-up talks in which the person speaking gets pretty convincing about the wisdom of living in the now, for several important reasons. One, it's all we've got. Two, we miss so much of what's good when we're pining away for our yesterdays (or tomorrows). Three, Jesus told us to live today and not to worry about tomorrow, because he has given us everything we need for just today. Bingo!

Oddly enough, it was the aloneness that finally got me to listen to what God had been telling me all along. Sure, I was at a crossroads, but even the most positive, promising changes bring a certain tension and some associated stress—because whether we admit it or not, we are creatures of habit. Habit comforts us. Habit makes it easier to plan our days without too much overthinking. Habits mold us and make us who we are.

So I decided that while my habits had to change, my emotions would eventually catch up with my new choices. In all truth, I still experience the occasional surges of sadness that our house is empty now. But most of the time, I'm too busy living in the moment and appreciating it for all it's worth.

Living in the moment isn't an optional choice we get to make in this life if we call ourselves Christians. It's a truly biblical mandate that Jesus instructs his followers to obey and take seriously. When we allow our thoughts to linger in the happy past (remember that we often forget the trying challenges of that "happy" past), we forfeit all the joys surrounding us today. When we continue to dream about the future (a future that hasn't been promised to any of us), we neglect the beauty of this day, this hour, this very minute.

Growing up and maturing means stepping out of the chaos of life long enough each day to reflect upon what we've learned along the way. It also means staying silent long enough for God to talk to us afresh, to direct (and redirect) our steps, and to infuse us with the desires he wants to fulfill in and through us.

Quietness might not be what we're used to after such long seasons of rearing children, but it might very well be the best thing for us. Sitting in his presence, waiting on him to nudge us, means we are confident he has some wonderful plans for us that will get our passions ignited in all the right ways. Certainly, as he has done all through the years, God has and always will set our feet in a spacious place. And that's his happy promise to us.

Take-away Action Thought

When my emotions get out of control and seemingly take on lives of their own, I will discipline myself to stop, sit, and listen.

My Heart's Cry to You, O Lord

Lord, you understand how much I sometimes hurt on the inside. No one else knows the emotional struggle I sometimes endure when I'm by myself and I start thinking about the way it used to be. This is wrong, Lord. Your word says that today is the day you have made, we should rejoice and be glad in it. I want that attitude and all its accompanying positive emotions to be at the forefront of my heart and mind. Today is a good day. Help me to stop before I head down the next pity-party tunnel, and instead give thanks to you for the wonderful memories I have. You are the One who sees my coming and going. I pray that I can listen well and then move into whatever you have next for me with gladness and joyful enthusiasm. Amen.

Chapter 6

Recognizing that Adult Children Make Adult-Sized Mistakes

Do not fret—it leads only to evil.
Psalm 37:8

Whatever you need is a stone's throw from what you fear.
Edward Welch

Some memories never completely lose the power of the emotional impact you felt when you first experienced the event. Good or bad, we all have specific moments in time we can never push to the periphery of our hearts and minds. Maybe it's a good thing to be able to recall such life-changing events—or then again, maybe not. I suppose it depends upon what you choose to do with the memory once it hits the forefront of your thoughts and refuses to be pushed aside.

Way back when, one of my children went through some five or so years of walking on the edge. I couldn't exactly tell you when we first started to notice that something was off, but once her choices grew so explosive it became glaringly obvious that she (and we) had a serious problem to contend with. There was the drinking, the partying, the financial losses, and then eventually trouble with the law.

While I can't tell you in exact detail what I was doing when we first heard about the drinking and driving and subsequent DUI, I can tell you how I felt. Undone. In denial. Overcome by fear. Worried sick. Yep, all these emotions literally dominated my thoughts and mind for many, many months.

I suppose the most telling moment came as I sat in a courtroom and watched my child walk to the front to face the judge. It was almost surreal. Sitting there among others who broke the law for any variety of reasons and their heartsick families made me want to weep, and I did. Once I got back into my car, the flood of tears let loose. There were so many conflicting thoughts and emotions running through my brain.

Anger. Check.
Disappointment. Check.
Sorrow. Check.
Doubt. Check.
Regret. Check.
Worry. Check.
Fear. Double-check.

Above all, I was afraid. Afraid my child hadn't learned her lesson. Afraid she would slip again and make more life-threatening mistakes. Afraid we wouldn't know how to help her. Afraid now that she was an adult she was almost completely beyond our control to . . . well . . . control.

That last and final fear was what kept me up at nights, worrying, praying, and worry-praying. I finally had to accept that there comes a day when parents do not have control over their children's actions. I saw firsthand what adult-sized mistakes looked like, felt like, and how they multiplied and entangled themselves into every segment of life (hers and ours). Physical. Emotional. Mental. Spiritual. Mistakes take no prisoners.

In my mother's heart, I wanted to be in control—no, *needed* to be in control. The irony is that the more I craved control to protect my child, the more I fretted, and when I fretted, I sinned. When I reacted in fear—controlling fear, that is—I wasn't living by faith, and my words and actions revealed that fact. It was only when I dropped to my knees before the Lord and pleaded with him to help me transfer ownership of my child to his care that I was able to let go.

And a beautiful, life-giving letting go it was. I let go of the responsibility to make my child do the right thing. I let go of imagining all the worst possible what-ifs that could happen. I let go of playing God in my child's life. And I'm still learning how to let go a little more day by day.

One of the principles by which we raised our children from babies onward was that they realized the value of being under our protection in every way possible. I recall countless times when my husband would gently remind our children that their choices would either protect them or place them in harm's way. When they heeded and honored our wishes for them in those early years, we were able to keep them from most danger. As they grew into teens, again, my husband reminded each of our children that while they had a lot more freedom, they needed to continue to use that freedom wisely.

When they made good choices, we rejoiced. When they erred, we drew them back and tried to help them rethink why they chose as they did. One conversation I recall in particular, because it struck me in a powerful way. Attempting to draw one child back from a rebellious attitude, my husband told her, "When you disobey and dishonor God's principles, you remove yourself from our protection, and we can't help you if you get into trouble outside of these four walls."

Sadly, that is exactly what occurred when one of our children ended up in court. In our home, we could dispense justice and mercy as we saw fit. Outside our home, the law of our state did so and without any mercy. In time, our daughter turned her life around, and today her testimony is built upon her past mistakes. Mercy and grace she knows firsthand, and so do we.

Take-away Action Thought

When I begin to worry and fear, I will remember that life and freedom fill me when I cast all my care at your feet.

My Heart's Cry to You, O Lord

You alone know the depth of my despair and fear when I scc my children making choices that will hurt them and dishonor you. I get so very anxious when I allow my fearful imagination to take over. Help me to focus on you alone, remembering that you love my child far more than I do. Give me the grace to realize that all I truly need in this life is your love, your presence, your empowering strength to meet every moment as a person of deep and abiding faith. I pray that you would continually watch over my children and draw them back to you if ever they stray. Amen.

Chapter 7

Welcoming Your Children's Future Dates and Mates

For you, God, have heard my vows;
you have given me the heritage of
those who fear your name.
Psalm 61:5

Sow a thought and you reap an action;
sow an action and you reap a habit;
sow a habit and you reap a character;
sow character and you reap a destiny.
Samuel Smiles

As I was driving home one day, on the radio were two medical doctors, who are also Christian counselors, talking about the challenges of starting, developing, and maintaining healthy relationships with one's adult children's future dates (and mates). As these two women alternately posed various troublesome scenarios, and then discussed possible solutions, it opened up a whole lot of questions for me personally. I kept driving, kept listening, and what I heard helped me flesh out some potential solutions if I should ever be in one of the situations they described.

As the week passed, I continued to mull over those issues they talked about in detail that had arisen multiple times in their medical practices/counseling sessions. Same story, different names, different faces.

One of these issues was dealing with our adult children's potential dates/mates. When they (the adult children) start bringing home potential dates/mates to meet the family, a good beginning makes all the difference in how the relationship develops. How parents choose to welcome their child's date/mate into their home for the first time is crucial, because first impressions make a huge impact on all of us. If we as the parents begin badly (for any variety of reasons), the possible future date/mate will have a difficult time overcoming that poor first meet/greet. They'll be hesitant to visit again—and naturally so.

Next, it is generally up to the parents to set the pace of the relationship and to be the ones who will open up the doors to their home and their hearts to the younger newcomer. Thus being relationally proactive is crucial if the parents expect to truly get to know their child's love interest on a level that will enable them to fully support the relationship, or perhaps offer a word or two of caution to their child.

Finally, even if things get off to a rough start, parents can (and should) make attempts at making amends, and offer opportunities to communicate openly (but kindly) about any misunderstandings or disagreements. None of us does something without a reason, for our actions relate to our own personal history. If we've had our own struggles with our in-laws, then we can relate to our child's future mate being fearful of the same scenario with us. Again, the burden is on us of proving to our children and their future mates that they won't have undue interference or be subject to manipulation after they marry.

In the end, making a good beginning is key, and we do so by sowing acts of kindness, goodness, and grace. Then we build upon that good start by consistently demonstrating respect and care, establishing a good habit. Finally, our own character is developed so that our actions predispose us (and our children) to a positive future and destiny, as it relates to their interaction with us if and when the relationship becomes permanent.

Of course, this whole issue of welcoming future dates/mates begs the obvious question of what parents should do when they cannot in good conscience support their child's decision to date/marry a particular person. The main consideration is to determine whether or not your objection is personal (meaning you simply don't care for the person based on personal preference), or you have a biblical objection (meaning that person doesn't share your faith in Jesus Christ and/or isn't living life as a disciple of Christ).

Personal preferences can be overcome with time, effort, and prayer. However, biblical objections need to be addressed using biblical principles and bathed in prayer before a conversation takes place with your child. Indeed, challenging your child, with love and respect of course, isn't an option for Christian parents. We have a responsibility to speak truth into our children's lives in all areas, as we do in our own, and this is especially important during relational decision-making time. It's not easy, and it may not be received well. But it isn't optional either. The same principles for getting to know our children's date/mate holds true as we initiate a serious conversation about marriage matters. Let it be bathed in prayer and then drenched in words of kindness, goodness, and grace.

Take-away Action Thought

When my children bring home their dates and future mates, I will take the initiative and gladly open my home and heart to get to know each of them.

My Heart's Cry to You, O Lord

Lord, I believe you will honor my prayer to bring my children into a relationship with the person you know is best for them. Marriage is a permanent covenant that is not to be entered into lightly. Help my children to recognize this truth first, and only then consider marrying someone who loves you more than them. I realize that my insight is limited and my ability to foresee the future is not available to me, which is why I rely on you, Lord, to guide and protect my children in all their relationships. Give me the good sense I require as my children introduce me to their choice in a spouse—and give me your kindness, goodness, and grace to serve this future mate in love. Amen.

Chapter 8

Recreating Your Life with Children on the Sidelines

For he has not despised or scorned
the suffering of the afflicted one.
Psalm 22:24

After all is said and done, more is said than done.
Anonymous

Conversations are important educators. Sometimes when we talk to people, we can walk away with profound insights we'll never forget. There is one conversation I remember with a woman I wouldn't have claimed to know well, until we spoke on a topic near and dear to her mother's heart one afternoon. Both of us were "catching up" and giving the other updates on our families when I noticed tears brimming in this woman's eyes. Before I even had the time to speak a word of comfort and concern, she told me why she was crying. "My kids are my life. They're my everything. Now that they're all out of the house I'm so depressed because I miss them so much. I can't help myself. I cry all day. I call them every single day just to make sure they're okay. It's not my fault; this is the way God made me."

If memory serves, it took me a few moments to process everything that had just spilled from her heart before I said anything. When I did speak, I admittedly held back because I didn't want to hurt this mother any more than she was already suffering. But I do recall agreeing with her that letting go and redefining our lives once our children grow up and move on was a real process. A grieving process. A process that takes time. A process that takes effort. Effort on our part.

It's on this point that this woman and I would diverge on how we choose to face our midlife, empty-nest parenting season. I agree that it does hurt sometimes, because we always miss those we love. However, I don't believe it's healthy (or wise) to make sure we call our children every day and check in just we as did when they were children and teens. Nor should we linger in a depressed emotional state for months on end because it's "how God made" us. God made parents with hearts that expand by the minute (and by the child) but we were *his* before we were parents. We are each a distinct individual handcrafted by God for our good and his glory, and he has glorious plans for our lives beyond our parenting role. Our parenting task technically may never end, but it certainly lightens up and changes as our children grow.

To stay stuck in a place where your only happiness in life comes when your children are front and center is wrong, nor should our children place us as their parents in the front and center of their lives. When our adult children leave home, we should view ourselves as parents with children on the sidelines of our lives. This—the sidelines, not the frontlines—is rightful place for them and for us. Admittedly, it isn't always easy to get ourselves into this position (mentally and functionally), but move we must. Our efforts and choices to fill our lives with other responsibilities, activities, and areas of service need to slowly take the central place in our lives. Do we neglect our children? Do we refuse to help them when needed? Do we grow lazy in loving our children? Never. The point is we can either wallow in what was or take active steps into what can be—it's our choice.

Inaction rather than action is a more common ailment than we might believe. Most people won't change until they get so uncomfortable that they are forced finally to do so. There is another way to live. Rather than living passively, and often miserably, why not take those action steps to a more fulfilling and satisfying existence?

If you won't do it for yourself, then consider your children. They love you. They want to see you happy because they love you. When you are mired in the past, how does that affect them? Children don't need parents who are overly dependent upon them. Adult children would be grateful beyond measure to know that their parents are doing well now that they have moved out and are busy with their own lives. Be that refreshing parent who is a joy to be with and who is flourishing, once your children have grown and gone. *This* is how God made us to live.

Take-away Action Thought

When I get stuck reliving the past, I will turn my attention to someone who needs my help today and then act on it.

My Heart's Cry to You, O Lord

Lord, most of the time I am completely content with where I am at in my life now. Then there are those "other" days when I can get completely caught up in life as it used to be when my children were younger. Honestly, I don't want to go back in time. I remember the difficulties and those moments when I often felt I couldn't wait until my children were just a little older. Parenting was hard at every stage of life (theirs and mine). Help me to see the beauty and the benefits of this season right now, today. Give me the vision to go after new and different goals. Lord, I rely on you to nudge me, open the doors you want me to walk through, and then equip me as I go. Day by day, I want to joyfully awaken each morning and expect you to accomplish great things in and through my life. Amen.

Chapter 9

Reinvesting in Your Marriage

You open your hand
and satisfy the desires of every living thing.
Psalm 145:16

Some couples who signed their wedding licenses twenty-five years ago have actually only been working on their marriages for about six months. They quit moving toward each other long ago.
Gary Thomas

Some years back, my husband's cousin sat talking with us about some changes she and her spouse were making in their lives. They have two children, both of whom were moving out and heading to college. This wise woman mentioned something in an off-handed way that she probably wouldn't ever remember but that I've never forgotten. Realizing that both she and her husband had given 110 percent to raising their sons and had made their world revolve around them, she also recognized that within one year they would be sitting across from each other in the kitchen eating dinner alone. Would they have anything left to talk about? Laugh about? Make decisions about? I could tell she had spent some time pondering this.

When she paused for a breath, this mother looked briefly at her husband and smiled as she turned back to me with these words, "I told him, pretty soon it's going to be just you and me." While some folks might take that statement like a death knell, the way my husband's cousin said it made me believe just the opposite. Already, they were planning on buying some property near a lake, getting a boat, and prepping (in the most fun-loving ways) for future grandchildren. More important, they were planning on doing it together. Planning. Dreaming. Doing. Together.

Looking back over the course of my married life, I know there have been seasons when my husband and I have barely held our heads above water trying to fulfill all our parental, vocational, and volunteer tasks. And in the real world that's how it really works. You have seasons where you put your all into just getting through the day. Then you have a stretch that feels a lot less stressful, more even-keeled, and thankfully much more relationship-building friendly. I think it helps to understand that highs/lows, intimacy/distance, serious/fun-loving are all part and parcel of a long-term relationship. A lot.

What also makes a difference is recognizing the truth that we were a couple first and then became parents. Our most important relationship is with our spouse. Since we rear our children to become independent enough to leave home for good, we ought to maintain and build our marriage all along the way. But do we? Inevitably, as my husband's cousin said, pretty soon it's going to be just you and your spouse. Either that concept makes you jump for joy, or you're scared to death. The upside is that what we do today can prepare us for tomorrow.

"For better or worse," and for everything in between, is what we promise on the day we get married. Of course, no amount of premarital counseling can prepare any of us for the challenges we sometimes face in marriage. Whether those difficulties are evidenced in parenting, finances, in-laws, health, jobs, or spiritual dimensioned differences, there will be hardships. Knowing this, and understanding that God uses the hard times to grow us up to become strong people of faith who don't falter when the slightest breeze hits us, we learn to accept the bad along with the good and work through it.

So should our attitude be toward our spouse. Over the span of time, we all change. Hopefully, we're all growing and resembling Christ's character in every thought, word, and deed. As we seek to honor God amid all the changes in life in general, let us place special emphasis on seeking an ever-growing intimacy with our spouse. With more time, energy, and availability, let us each put daily effort into knowing our spouse more deeply, asking the important questions, and reacquainting ourselves with their preferences/dislikes if we've forgotten. Most of all, let every day be a new opportunity to make our spouse glad we said "I do" all those years ago.

Take-away Action Thought

In the coming weeks and months, remind me to take pen and paper and make time to sit with my spouse to plan for our future (and fun) together.

My Heart's Cry to You, O Lord

Father, it's been quite some time since I've done any planning with only my spouse in mind. Help us to both get excited about dreaming together and expectantly spending time alone now that our children have grown. Remind us that as we spend time talking, praying, and enjoying each other's company, our children have a greater sense of security and stability no matter how old they are. No longer do we necessarily have to offer our children a home, but we can always provide them with two parents who love and respect each other, and who are committed to make it through everything life throws at us. Lord, you alone can cement our love in a way that endures all trials. Protect our relationship and give us the strength to die to ourselves so that we can lift each other up in love. Amen.

Chapter 10

Viewing Your Adult Children as Peers and Equals

Spread your protection over them.
Psalm 5:11

Before I got married I had six theories about bringing up children; now I have six children and no theories.
John Wilmont

I have a working theory and I'm sticking to it. We are and always will be, in large part, a product of our mistakes. That doesn't necessarily need to be a bad thing. In fact, if we've taken the opportunity to learn from our errors, then we're sure to come out on the plus side every time. Think of mistakes this way. They are sure elements of our everyday life, so we'd better make peace with that truth. Some mistakes are of the small variety where all we need to do is pick ourselves up, brush ourselves off, and keep on moving forward. But I'm thinking here of those gnashing-teeth, forever life-altering types of errors that beat you to the ground.

And let's be honest, we've all created such messes for ourselves at one time or another. When we reflect back upon those time-stopping, heart-pounding moments, we wonder if we've truly ruined our lives for good (or more accurately, for bad). But if we believe that our lives are ruined forever, we haven't been paying close enough attention to what God's word says about making mistakes, asking forgiveness, making reparation, and moving on.

Even with my now sometimes muddied-up middle-aged memory, I can summon up far too many times when I spoke or acted rashly and ended up regretting both my words and my actions. I also realize, however, that through the undoing of each error I changed. I learned how to ask for help from those wiser than myself. I learned what true humility means when I had to go and ask for forgiveness from someone I injured. I learned what it means to reflect back on a mistake (though not in a morose way) to identify what I did wrong, and why, and make sure not to make the same poor choice a second (or twentieth!) time.

Which is why I'm still asking myself why I feel compelled to interfere in my adult children's lives when I see them venturing into territory where they might get hurt. I'm not talking about their blatant sinful choices, when it is always right and appropriate to step in and steer another toward a righteous path. Rather, I'm thinking of those decisions where personal preference would lead me in a way that's different from the way my children are taking. It could be financial, relational, vocational, or even health-related.

If I'm sticking to my theory that we are all a product of our mistakes, why am I so opposed (and short-sighted) that I don't want my children making mistakes I could help them avoid? In the long run, I hope against hope that all of my children (and yours) have a faith that is robust enough to counter every misstep along the path of life. Part of that strength comes only when we fail, set it right, and then keep going. I believe that this quality is called perseverance.

Your mistakes and mine will either be the making or the breaking of us—likewise with our children, no matter what their age. I've come to realize that while I daily pray for God to protect my children from every sort of harm (including making poor decisions), I must follow through that prayer with an addendum: *Lord, help my children to turn straight back to you after they make a mistake. Fill them through and through with a humble, teachable heart that seeks to honor you above all. Give them the strength they need to ask for forgiveness, make reparations, and then get right back up with the grace you supply. Amen.*

Sometimes parents need someone to remind them of their many mistakes from years gone by and what they learned from making them—not that it will ever be easy on a parent's heart to watch or anticipate the potential pain their children will experience if they head down a path we know is best to avoid.

The truth is, perhaps it isn't always the best (at least, in the long run) for our children to avoid that certain path we're wringing our hearts and hands over day and night. Sometimes, a spanking from the school of life at age twenty might be enough of a deterrent so that they never go down that particular road again. When we choose rescue over wisely stepping back and praying, we often thwart what God is trying to teach our children. If I persist in playing Rescue Mom throughout their young adult years, what will happen when my children hit a crisis I cannot fix?

Instead of fretting and fuming over choices our children opt for—choices we would avoid with all our middle-aged wisdom and experience—how about committing them daily to our all-knowing, all-powerful, all-loving heavenly Father? He understands far better than we ever will how each little detour along their spiritual journey through life will affect them (for good or bad). And let's be honest, we wouldn't step in and tell our peers how to handle every decision in their life, would we? As we place increasingly more trust in God, we'll find it easier to find the grace to view our children as peers and equals.

Take-away Action Thought

When I see my children making choices I wouldn't make, I will step back, say a prayer, and resist the urge to react with emotionally charged words.

My Heart's Cry to You, O Lord

Here I am again, Lord, coming to you with a request for the strength to not allow my imagination to run wildly as I anticipate disaster for my children. Help me to remain calm and collected when my children inform me of their most recent decisions. Give me the self-control to speak only when asked for advice, or when you prompt me to do so. I need your eternal perspective. Your wisdom and understanding are what I plead for when I become anxious and afraid for my children. O Lord, please spread your blanket of protection over my children and upon every decision they make. Amen.

Chapter 11

Twisting the Plot—You're a Grandparent

He decreed statutes for Jacob
and established the law in Israel,
which he commanded our ancestors
to teach their children,
so the next generation would know them,
even the children yet to be born,
and they in turn would tell their children.
Psalm 78:5–6

Successful parenting is the rightful, God-ordained loss of control. The goal of parenting is to work ourselves out of a job.
Paul Tripp

I was sitting in the passenger's seat of my car and my eldest daughter was driving when she told me the news of her first pregnancy. I was so happy. So, so happy. Those first few days I felt like I was walking on air as wonderful memories flooded my mind about my own firsts in parenting way back when. I could remember holding my daughter for the first time, and each subsequent "first" that followed, until I had an entire panoramic movie running through my brain. It was bliss.

Yes, I was happy—and then suddenly I wasn't. That free-floating sense of all being right in the world gave way to a free-floating fear that reasserted itself at the oddest times. At first, I thought something must be wrong with me. I loved my children and was thrilled my daughter was having her own baby. So why was I afraid?

Then I figured it out. All those happy first memories of mine had given way to the reality of parenting—such as staying up all night trying to decide just how sick your child is. Or those moments when I felt I didn't have the answers my child needed or the wisdom to find them. Especially those moments when I felt so out of control I thought I would never experience a full night's sleep again, never ever.

Yes, I was happy—until I wasn't. No one ever told me I might expect to feel some of the very same emotions, fears, and struggles as a grandmother-to-be that I went through the first time as a mother. Here I was at fifty years old, my own children were in their twenties, and I was experiencing flashbacks of my darker (and even desperate) parenting moments. I wondered to myself if I could handle going through the highs/lows of parenting a second time, even as a grandparent.

Not that we have any choice in the matter—but once that scary thought surfaces, we have to face it. It was an interesting nine months of preparation time for me. While my daughter's tummy grew larger and larger, my fears seemed to diminish accordingly. I began watching my first child make preparations for her first child and it heartened me. I started pushing back any anxious thoughts in order to embrace the possibilities this new life would hold. Instead of allowing my mind to retreat into the shadowy places where my personal insecurities and fears thrive best, I brought them into the open and shared my concerns with a trusted friend who talked me off the ledge and then prayed for me. Bringing these fears to light helped to free me from them once and for all.

Interestingly, I'm not the only mother who's experienced this sudden feeling of being overwhelmed when her adult child announces a baby is on the way. The more openly I talked about my fears, the more other women shared similar stories. I suppose becoming a grandparent follows the same principle as parenting: We have to go into it knowing that if we do the task as God ordained, then we'll be working ourselves out of a job and giving up control all along the way.

I've now been a grandmother for some years now, and I can say that all my anxieties melted away the moment I held my first grandson. As for those fears, I couldn't tell you where they went. I'm too busy working myself out of a job with my grandchildren.

Of course, we'd all appreciate a redo on certain junctures of our lives when we made poor choices, spoke out of turn, or even held back rather than move into something new because we were afraid.

One of the best aspects of being a grandparent is that you're just enough removed from the dailies of parenting that you can sometimes see problems (and their solutions) more clearly than the sleep-deprived, exhaustion-ridden parents. This is a good thing. Given that we all need a better perspective when times get rough, grandparents can offer a more hopeful one each and every time it's needed.

Another wonderful part of grandparenting is being close enough to lend a hand, pray a little prayer (or a long intense one), offer a reprieve and babysit, and just generally be the steady ones who don't overreact, but instead give voice to that fact that parenting is an ongoing process of growth for the whole family. Ready. Set. Grow!

Take-away Action Thought

I will look for ways to be the grandparent who invests in my grandchild's life physically, mentally, emotionally, and spiritually.

My Heart's Cry to You, O Lord

Father, help me to trust you to supply me with all I need to be the kind of grandparent you want to me to be. Give me your wisdom and strength to serve, love, and point these precious little people to you. I need your constant guidance in my life, so that I don't grow into a fearful grandparent who spends more time worrying for her family than praying for them. Give me your eternal perspective on all things, and give me the opportunity to pass that on to my children. Thank you, Lord, for new life—and the endless possibilities that every baby brings to this world. Amen.

Chapter 12

Stepping in to Parent Your Grandchildren in a Crisis

"Those who sacrifice thank offerings honor me."
Psalm 50:23

Friend, it is God's responsibility to supply what you require. Your duty is to trust Him, obey Him, and keep your focus on Him.
Charles Stanley

It was 3:40 a.m. when a creaking door woke me up and a timid four-year-old voice told me it was "time to get up." I almost jumped out of my skin. The third time my grandson did this, I put him in the bed with me and told him to be quiet—desperately trying to keep his younger brother, who was sleeping in his crib next to my bed, from waking up. After about two hours of being kicked in the back and asked every few minutes if it was time to get up (it wasn't), I gave in. At precisely 5:30 a.m., my grandson and I were up making scrambled eggs for Grandpa—while I, still bleary-eyed, stumbled about to make some coffee for a quick, mind-clearing caffeine fix.

Several hours later, grandson number two woke up all smiles, and I repeated the preparations for another hot breakfast for him. By 9:30 a.m., I most resembled a walking zombie. At 11:30 a.m., my daughter arrived to retrieve her sons, and I immediately collapsed onto the couch for a short reprieve. It took me the better part of that day to recover physically from a single sleepless night.

All that to say, when I finally regained enough energy to get busy working at my computer, one e-mail in my inbox caught my attention and held it. For about two years now, a good friend of mine and his wife have had custody of their granddaughter, a four-year-old girl about to enter preschool. As I read their prayer request/update that involved specific legal issues surrounding their case to gain permanent legal custody of their granddaughter, I reflected upon their horrific journey and wondered if I would have strength (physically, that is) to rear one of my grandchildren if a catastrophe ever occurred in our family.

My friend's situation is every parent's nightmare, because their child was in part responsible for injuries their grandchild suffered before being removed from her home. I recalled the frightening details of the case, and how shocked my friend and his wife were to discover how their darling young granddaughter had been ill-treated. Worse still, they posed the question everyone was asking: Why did the father allow his wife to mistreat this innocent child for as long as she did?

There were no good answers. Instead, lots of questions and accusations accompanied the call to take their granddaughter home immediately (and for the foreseeable future).

This was what my friend did (and is still doing). Like me, these grandparents are in their fifties, and neither ever expected to begin the parenting journey all over again. And yet they are parenting 24/7, despite their age, their exhaustion, their unknowns, and in spite of the grief they live with every single day.

It is clear from speaking with this couple that despite the uncertain future they face with their son and his wife, and with their granddaughter's custody battle, they have placed their trust in God's provision alone. In fact, both of them can be heard praising the Lord for putting them in the right place at the right time for the benefit of their beloved granddaughter. They realize things could have gone very differently and a tragic ending for the child could have been a real possibility.

So they trust. They give thanks. Even on sleepless mornings when they experience what I did with my grandson, they turn their attention to the Lord, ask him for provision for the day, and keep on going. It's a mind-blowing, faith-growing, ongoing miracle in the making to everyone who knows this couple. Is it easy? Nope. Is it without frequent disappointments and hardships? No indeed. But they don't allow these setbacks to get in the way of loving their granddaughter. Crisis or no crisis, they know God is in this and will keep them strong through it.

Given how unpredictable life is, it's my belief that the best way to prepare for the worst is to know what you believe, and in whom you believe, well before tragedy strikes. Once we're mired in the pain of an event so horrific and dumbfounding, we don't have the mental clarity to begin the process of working through the faith issues we had taken for granted during smoother times.

No one can see what tomorrow will bring. Rather than worry ourselves sick over what might happen tomorrow or next year, wouldn't it make a whole lot more sense to transform our uncertainties into confidence in God who is certain? Of course, preparedness might look different to one person than to another. But God is clear on one subject: we need to have our minds renewed each and every day. So take some time daily to sit yourself down in a solitary spot to read, reflect, pray, and give thanks to our great God who promises to provide for our every need, every hour, every day. It's what he does best.

Take-away Action Thought

On those days when I feel overwhelmed and underprepared to offer help to my family, I will call to mind the promises of your provision. Then I will step forth and do what needs doing.

My Heart's Cry to You, O Lord

Lord, there are some aspects of being a grandparent that I never anticipated or expected. Remind mc in my moments of doubt that you are my Provider and that my job is only to trust and obey you. Give me the courage to intervene when I'm called to do so, and to take on extra responsibility when it is clear you are leading me there. Help me one day at a time to serve you and my family with grace, strength, and love. Enable me to put even the most hurtful situations directly into your healing and always capable hands. Keep reminding me that you are well able to work miracles anywhere, anytime. Thank you, Lord, for giving me the opportunity to meet a need and the strength required to complete the task. Amen.

Chapter 13

Building Good Relationships with Your Children's In-Laws

LORD Almighty,
blessed is the one who trusts in you.
Psalm 84:12

Gratitude is not the quiet game. It begs to be expressed, both to God and to others. "Silent gratitude," Gladys Berthe Stern said, "isn't much use to anyone."
Nancy Leigh DeMoss

You may have enjoyed a marvelous meet-and-greet with your adult son's or daughter's soon-to-be in-laws. Or not. I've heard, though I've never experienced it, that some of the first time meetings with future in-laws can get pretty dicey. And why not?

To be realistic, it takes a lot of diversity to make our world go round, and we're often drawn to something (or someone) who is refreshingly different from us. I'm not talking about core beliefs and a strong moral code. Rather, I'm suggesting (because it's true!) that people and their families are like tiny microcosms of communities, all with their own set of rules and regulations they live and die by.

Every one of us has our own unwritten but viable list of dos and don'ts by which we govern our lives. Since we all crave a sense of order to make life simpler, we learn from our grandparents and our parents how to do "life." Then, we marry and create our own miniature society with our spouse and subsequent children.

Quite innocently, our children unconsciously absorb these ideals and attempt to transfer them to their adult relationships. And there's the rub. Whether or not our family house rules make sense, they make sense to us. The same holds true for our young adult children's future spouses and their families.

Which is why attitude is everything. Finding that single area of common ground at the first possible opportunity can break the relational ice in the warmest way imaginable. Then building upon said common ground is the next wise step to learning how this other side of the family lives, learns, and loves. Never underestimate how important a good start can be to creating a sound foundation for a mutually respectful long-term relationship.

And because parents are the ones who've already learned how to get along with their own in-laws over the years, they frequently have to take the lead in guiding their own adult children in developing a heartfelt spirit of openness, humility, and gratitude.

Why gratitude? When our hearts are wise enough to see the blessings when others miss them, then we have hearts that have honed an inner spirit of thanking God for everything in our lives—the good, the bad, and even the ugly. We aren't looking for perfection in any person, place, or thing. Instead, we give thanks for the opportunity to express God's love to those who might very well look quite unusual or strange to our eyes. We encourage our adult children to look for some common ground and build from there, so that we can learn from them and vice versa. Give and take. Then give and give some more, which leads to thanks for the gift of getting to know the very ones who gave life to and then reared the son- or daughter-in-law to whom our children have pledged their lives for all their days.

Attitude is everything. Learning to discipline our hearts and minds to be thankful in all circumstances (because God allowed them) and for every person in our life (because God placed them there) is simple obedience.

We can gripe and complain for years on end when we don't like the way others do things, or how they treat us, but it only spoils us and destroys any hope for a new start or reconciliation. God expects us to trust him enough to give us the good grace to love even those in our lives we may not like. As we obey him, we can excel at overcoming differences, distances, and disagreements. He meets us more than halfway by supernaturally equipping us to serve others in love. Perhaps in time, we will have the ultimate joy and honor of introducing those we struggle to understand to the One who loves us best.

First, we commit the relationship to the care and keeping of God. Next, we find areas of common ground and build from there. Then we pray earnestly for God to keep opening doors of opportunity to demonstrate in practical ways how much we love them. What chance does anyone have at resisting such love for long?

Take-away Action Thought

Whenever I feel judgmental or displeased by someone I don't understand or agree with, I will purposefully bring to mind an area of common ground and build upon it.

My Heart's Cry to You, O Lord

Help me, Lord, at the very beginning of any new relationship to look for the best in others. Give me your eyes to recognize and appreciate the uniqueness in those different from myself. Help me to discover their areas of giftedness and look for ways to compliment them appropriately. Too often, I'm taken by surprise when someone isn't like me, and I tend to shy away instead of pursuing a friendship with him or her. This is not right and I need your gentle nudging to keep me on track. In all things, Lord, I need to give thanks and trust you to equip me to love the people you bring into my life. For their good and your glory, I rely upon your grace to do so. Amen.

Chapter 14

Redefining Your Role in Life Now

All my longings lie open before you, Lord;
my sighing is not hidden from you.
Psalm 38:9

Hope is not a granted wish or a favor performed; no, it's far greater than that. It's a zany, unpredictable dependence on a God who loves to surprise us out of our socks and be there in the flesh to see our reaction.
Max Lucado

Life is always in motion. Once you take a step in any direction, you simply cannot go back again. I thank the good Lord for that truth, for the most part. Then there are those other times when I wish I could rewind the clock for a redo or an undo, or possibly a brief peek into the future. If I'm honest, many of my parenting years were spent not knowing what was around the next corner. So why do I feel the great need to know what's next for me now that my children are grown?

All parents find out soon enough (if they hadn't already discovered that principle immediately after they get married) that once their child is born life is rarely, if ever, the neat and tidy Christmas card-like depiction they hoped for and planned on. It simply isn't. Rather, life is mostly messy, tiresome, often hopelessly a daily grinding away at the same tasks morning and night, but also full of the unexpected.

By design, I believe parenting, like life, is meant to keep moms and dads on their knees and fully dependent upon God, his word, and generous measures of hope. It is hope that can burn most brightly amid the darkest storms or dimmest slivers of unwanted and tragic unknowns. Parents, by nature, hope for many things. We hope our children don't come to any danger, terrible illnesses, bad relationships, financial distress, and so on. Above all, we hope our children come to a saving relationship with Jesus Christ early on, because we know how tough life can get and we know how much we lean on Jesus alone.

As my own children have grown, I've come to realize that along with all the hoping for the best for my children, I've had to summon up some pretty hefty doses of hope for myself too. No longer is the majority of my time and energy spent actively parenting. Instead, on occasion, I sometimes find myself with a little time to spare, and I look around the corners of my house half-expecting (half-hoping?) to see a swarm of noisy children running past me. To what? Save me? Distract me? Complete me? Hopeless, isn't it?

I've found that while I can be happy my children are now adults and living full lives outside these four walls, I'm still reeling a bit from the emotional adjustment and lagging behind sometimes. I suppose this might be one reason why so many folks struggle during midlife and endure personal seasons of crises—they are simply running to catch up with their newest and ever-evolving role in life. Surprise!

Who am I now that I've reared my children to adulthood? How do I spend the time I once invested in them? What are my deepest desires and dreams? How should I best put my gifts and talents to use? These are just a few questions I've asked myself during my quieter moments. Truth be told, some days I'm not quite sure of what to expect. But always, my great hope lies in the fact that God knows. He sees my longings, hears my sighs, and gently reminds me that he has good surprises just around the next corner. He does, for sure and certain.

There's hope and then there's real hope—the kind of hope you can sink your heart and mind and even teeth into because you *know*. You know that God has this whole season of life worked out. From the beginning of time, God knew how life would play out for you and for me. He knew that with each season of life there would be changes (inside of us and outside around us), and that life would always be in motion. It's not a bad thing unless we've become so comfortable in our yesterdays that we don't want to step into our tomorrows.

Although we can't see our future, we can see how the unchanging, amazing faithfulness of God is testified to throughout the Bible. We can trust our uncertain futures because we serve a certain God. Even when we feel our identities have been stripped away, God will remind us of our permanent identity as his chosen children. No matter how shaken we may feel today, God is there with us. Leading us, challenging us, nudging us, to see clearly that he holds all things in his hands—even me, even you, even our next starring roles handpicked by him who knows us best of all.

Take-away Action Thought

When I see my life changing before my eyes, I will remember that you are the God of change and that all you do is good.

My Heart's Cry to You, O Lord

Father, help me to realize that every day is a day ripe with opportunities to see you work in my life for the good of others. Give me a calm spirit, unshakable despite the changes that surround me and those I love. Keep working in the deepest levels of my heart, Lord, and give me courage to step forward into whatever is next for me. I thank you for my family and all the years we had together in our home. I thank you even more for the hope I feel spring up in my heart as I anticipate great things ahead. Amen.

Chapter 15

Letting Adult Children Become Fiscally Responsible

Whom have I in heaven but you?
And earth has nothing I desire besides you.
Psalm 73:25

It is easier to suppress the first desire than to satisfy all that follow it.
Benjamin Franklin

Many years ago, I sat with a group of young women doing a book study together. One of them started to complain that she was certain she knew what God wanted her to do with her life, but she lacked the money to make it happen. To this day, I remember what the group leader said in answer to this woman's complaint: "Money is one of God's tools that he uses to guide our steps. If he gives you money, he has a purpose for it. If he withholds funds, he has a purpose for that too." After that, we enjoyed a lively discussion about money and the real world.

As we talked about our own personal money frustrations, it was a common theme that everyone at one time or another struggles with the power money wields. It was also apparent that most folks feel they never have enough of "it," whatever "it" may be—money, time, energy, the list goes on. But we also realized that when it comes right down to it, God promises to provide for our needs, not our ever-expanding list of wants and indulgences. This truth, then, begs the question of how we differentiate between the two—needs and wants—and how we can live in such a way that money isn't our taskmaster, so that our children learn the biblical way to handle it as well.

The more I think back on this conversation, the more I realize that God's word gives us all the guidance we require to handle money in the appropriate manner—and it all begins with the heart. If we treasure God first and foremost, then all our other desires will fall into place. If we treasure stuff more than God, then all our other desires will be out of whack. One on one with God, each of us needs to ask some hard questions, and be ready for God to prompt us to make some changes if need be.

How does this principle of finance affect us as parents of grown adults? Like every other area of parenting, our children are paying close attention to how we make "material" decisions in life. How do we prioritize our spending? Are we in debt because our wants went beyond our paychecks? Do we owe money to our lenders (banks/friends/family)? Do we tithe first, and honor God by trusting him to care for us? Do we give generously to others when needs are made known? Do we save a portion each month as wise stewards?

All these questions need valid answers, and if we are somewhat embarrassed by our past choices, then there's never a better time to make amends than today. As Ben Franklin said, "It is easier to suppress the first desire than to satisfy all that follow it." Our first priority is to bend the knee (and our wallet) before the Almighty and seek his wisdom on all money matters. Then we put into daily practice the wise guidance found in Scripture. Only when we handle money in a way that honors God can our children learn how to handle their own cash rightly.

If you're like me, you know some empty-nest parents who are still bailing their adult children out of financial messes. Some parents I know tell me they do so because they didn't set the best example for their children growing up and, sadly, their children are failing with their finances in the same way their folks did and may be still doing. Other parents continue to pass the buck (literally), because they feel guilty if their children seem to suffer because they don't enjoy the same level of income and lifestyle, which took their parents a lifetime of hard work and good stewardship to build. Neither excuse benefits the children over the long term.

Instead of giving in to the emotional response of the moment, it would be far more loving to step back from the situation and to pray, get counsel from other parents, and then consider practical ways to equip the child to make sound financial choices from there on out. Real love sometimes means allowing the painful consequences of impulsive spending or poor money management to leave its mark.

There is a reason why God "disciplines" those he loves—he wants to spare us further, and more severe, pain later on in life. Parents need to pay attention to the way God loves best. It isn't necessarily by opening up the heavens and scattering the skies with more money, if we haven't already learned how to handle what we've been given in the past.

Take-away Action Thought

When I see my children struggling with money issues, I will resist my first impulse to step in and rescue them. Instead, I will pray, get counsel, and make a plan of action to equip them to make sound decisions.

My Heart's Cry to You, O Lord

Lord, help me to truly understand your way of handling money so I can, by example, teach my children how they should view and use this tool in the most effective way possible. Help us to never place money in the position of an idol where we begin to trust in our cash more than we trust in your perfect provision. Give us daily wisdom and the self-control to say no to impulse spending so we don't end up in financial debt. Lord, if we ever find ourselves in the sad position of having to watch our children suffer for their poor financial choices, give us your divine guidance and eternal perspective on how to best help them through their crisis. Above all, may we desire you first and foremost. Amen.

Chapter 16

Reinventing Life Goals from Midlife and Beyond

Like a tree planted by streams of water,
which yields its fruit in season
and whose leaf does not wither—
whatever they do prospers.
Psalm 1:3–4

I will not just live my life. I will not just spend my life. I will invest my life.
Helen Keller

A friend's husband walked out on her and their three preschool children, leaving her feeling that her life and future as she knew it had ended. Then, over time, she began again, accomplishing goals she never even considered while she was married. She earned a bachelor's degree, continued on for a master's degree, and then started her own online business. I'm so proud of her and so thankful to have this remarkable woman in my life—and even better, she's my best friend.

I had a close-up, intimate perspective on what she had to do to overcome the special challenges of becoming a suddenly single mom, who had previously spent her hours and days as a stay-at-home mother. To say her entire life had been upended would literally be true. Slowly, she regained her bearings and started to rebuild all the broken places inside of her heart, as well as to lead her young family to a place of inner healing.

It took years, yes. The point being my friend didn't allow her ex-husband's poor choices to determine her future or to become her identity. God remade her from the inside out, and she led her children to the only One who can set us free from abandonment, shame, guilt, and every other dead-end road. While my friend's journey was certainly a painful one, when she reflects back on those early years, she sees God's hand of provision and grace all over them. She knows she couldn't have gotten to where she is today without him and his guiding hand.

While many of us midlifers won't have the dramatic personal history of overcoming such amazing odds as my friend, we too have a challenge of sorts right before us—and it can feel daunting. How many of us ever look further than our immediate set of responsibilities to dream a little dream anymore? How many of us truly believe that God can do something amazing and surprising through our efforts even now? How many of us even bother to inquire of the Lord anymore about our future?

During our younger parenting decades, when we focused on being the best parents we could be, none of us had much more time or energy (physical or mental) to spare for dreaming about fulfilling those long put-off goals. We naturally sacrificed many of our pursuits for our family's well-being and have no regrets about doing so. Today, however, we're sitting in a different place and time. We now have the skill-set, the experience, the maturity, and possibly some of the same dreams and goals as we did so long ago. But what to do with them?

One word comes to mind as we enter that empty-nest/midlife season. Invest. Invest ourselves fully and never stop. We shouldn't be content to coast into our silver years. Rather, we need to summon up the courage to do something bold for God, while we still have the physical and mental strength to make it happen. Invest. Start today by inquiring of the Lord, and then listen to his gentle nudges. Watch for doors of opportunity to open, and then take the first step and walk through them.

I cannot count the number of times I've heard the clarion call from pastors across our nation when they speak on aging. What is this call to arms? It is to stop living lives in a comfortable complacency just because you can. Instead, do an about-face, turn your heart and mind to your Commander-in-Chief, and start obeying his marching orders. As these pastors remind us, if you're still alive and breathing, then the Lord has something of importance for you to accomplish; otherwise, he'd take you to heaven.

When said that way, I feel a shaking deep down inside of me that simply cannot refuse to heed God's call on my life—no matter how old I am. Even if I am bewildered about what to do, I can look around me and begin meeting the needs of those closest to me faithfully, daily, and gratefully. As I serve in practical ways today, God may fling open a completely new door tomorrow. The point being, I cannot justify wasting my hours and days away because I don't yet have a clear direction.

As my friend learned during her grief-stricken newness to single parenting, it is enough to faithfully carry out the responsibilities closest to her one day at a time. Then, in time, God miraculously opens new doors and prepares us to serve him there. One final word: God calls those who have made themselves available, and then he equips them to carry out his instructions. Trust and obey, there's no other way.

Take-away Action Thought

I will refuse to live my life in complacency, and I will make plans to invest myself and my resources into the lives of those around me as God directs.

My Heart's Cry to You, O Lord

Father, I admit that I've been so used to seeing myself as a parent to my children that I've forgotten you might have something more for me now that they are grown. I don't want to waste these years resting comfortably just because I can. Help me to press forward into the next season of life with excitement and positive expectancy. Guide my heart to hear what you would have me do. Give me your wisdom and direction as you open up new avenues for service and accomplishment. Keep reminding me that as long as I have breath, you have an assignment for me to fulfill. Amen.

Chapter 17

Helping Adult Children Endure the Difficult Seasons of Life

I will not die but live,
and will proclaim what the LORD has done.
Psalm 118:17

Something powerful happens when we shift the weight of our expectations away from the fulfillment of our own dreams and set it fully on the God of all dreams.
Bo Stern

Short-sighted, shallow-faithed person that I am at times, I don't immediately see the benefits of suffering—my own or my children's. I forget that the large part of who I am today is because of the rough patches I've endured. Still, when I see my child in pain, there's nothing I want more than to end their hurt. It's no wonder God chose not to equip mothers with the supernatural power to reach out and simply point their finger at the culprit of pain and reduce it (or them) to ashes.

We laugh, but the sentiment is all too true. As parents we spend the bulk of our lives taking measure after measure to protect our children from harm. We learn, over the years, how to be quite skillful at it—experts, in the truest sense of the word, given that it takes approximately 10,000 hours for an individual to master a skill. Then our children grow up and move out of our jurisdiction of protection, but nobody told us how hard it would be to step back and do nothing in response to their tearful cries (or not so subtle cues) for help.

Rather than bemoan the injustice of this life transition into the empty-nest parenting stage, it would be much more effective if we reminded ourselves that no one grows during the high times of life. It's during those stretching seasons of difficulty that we all develop into the man or woman God has designed for us to become, so that we're able to fulfill his plan for our lives.

Since we can't take away our children's tough seasons of life (and we shouldn't want to), we should first gently remind ourselves, and then our children, that God is in the business of breaking us down to build us stronger than ever. Why not act as sideline cheerleaders who take note of the growth in maturity, the responses of trusting faith, and the spirit of humility we see developing in our children as they learn to endure tough times? These kindly spoken words of encouragement will enable our children to face difficulties with the biblical perspective that God never wastes pain. He will use it to remake us over and over again into the image of his Son.

One of our most prevalent parental fears is that our child will not survive their current crisis. We, with our tender parental hearts, view the situation as unthinkably cruel, and we fret away the days (and nights) worrying over our children's abilities to handle life's hardships.

We forget that everyone endures seasons of life's pain and suffering, and that our task is now to bring a word of encouragement, hope, and faith to the situation. As we help our adult children see the traumatic situation through the lens of eternity and faith, these hard times can be pared down to a more manageable problem. As we lend our listening ear, make practical suggestions, and offer what assistance we can, our children will be more fully equipped to deal with and eventually make it through whatever they face.

The bottom line is that God knows exactly how much pressure to apply to our lives, in depth and duration, for it to remake us from the inside out. Over time, we can and will look back long enough to glean all the sweetness from even the bitterest of experiences. When we do, we'll live to tell others of God's faithfulness.

Take-away Action Thought

When I become afraid for my children,
I will reflect back on God's faithfulness
to me during my times of testing, and I
will put pen to paper listing each event
that built my faith for today's crisis.

My Heart's Cry to You, O Lord

In the morning hear my cry to you, Lord. I come to you with a heavy heart and a broken spirit. You know the situation our family is facing. You already know its outcome. Help us to continue to rely on your strength each day and not to worry about the future. Give me the words to say to my children that will bring hope and encouragement to them as they face these difficulties. Help them to remember that you will never forsake them and that you have promised to supply all their needs. Give us the wisdom to remember that you build us up as we endure tough times. Give us glimpses along the way that you are indeed changing all of us from the inside out. Amen.

Chapter 18

Having Fun—Even When Your Adult Children Have Problems

My heart is steadfast, O God;
  I will sing and make music with all my soul.
Psalm 108:1

We must not forget His benefits while dealing with our problems. Even before His answer is in sight, thank Him—for being there, for listening, for working all things according to His will.
Nancy Leigh DeMoss

"We need to do something fun," says the one parent. Pause. Wait for it. Here it comes. The other parent's reply, "But what about . . ."—insert the description of your adult child's most current problem. It would be funny, if it weren't true.

We live with our hearts and minds always hovering over the general vicinity of our children's present zip code. When one child is hurting, most parents can't think about much else until their child gets through the worst of it. They worry. They think (and overthink). Then they ruminate on the problem verbally with their spouse (or a trusted friend) until the other finally says, "Enough already!"

I've been told many times over the years that I seem to be regressing into anxiety the older my children grow. Admittedly, I try to defend myself, but my husband is right. Once again it's the old truism of "little kids = little problems; big kids = big problems." We feel the brunt of this every single day, and in the process we forfeit the joy (and the joyful, fun-loving times) God has placed in our paths.

We're wrong when we put the brakes on our own lives to instead fret over our children's problems. I remind myself that while I might get the two confused at times, every person has two circles in their lives. One is the circle of responsibility: it's generally small and includes a spouse, children, and other family members. The second circle is the circle of care: it's much larger and usually includes (but is not limited to) those found in the circle of responsibility, but with a big difference. We can care about a lot of people and issues, and do our best to alleviate these problems, but we are not responsible to do so. We're to care, not carry.

The difference is significant as our children grow up, because they slowly move into the outer circle of care rather than stay inside the circle of responsibility. As they grow up and grow out of our responsibility circle, we continue to care for them, but we are no longer responsible for fixing every one of their problems. Again, how we express our parental love begins to change.

Since life is always lived with dual pain and pleasure, there will rarely be a single day when everything is right in the world at large (or in our children's lives). So when do parents of adult children decide they can take a break from their children's problems and go have fun?

Excellent question. For most parents, the answer is "Today." Even though our children may be mired in some tough situations, we have to place them in God's faithful hands to care for and to protect. As we strengthen our trust in God to do so, we can be free to hand over the reins of responsibility in favor of lovingly caring from the sidelines and having a little fun ourselves. Yes, it is possible to do a little happy dance even before the problem is solved. In fact, a bit of spontaneous fun may even spark some solutions to the problems at hand. Who knew having fun could have a dual purpose?

Many years ago, a friend who is farther along in the parenting journey than I am passed along a piece of wisdom I've never forgotten. This mother of five children and seven grandchildren told me that as her children moved out of state and scattered across the country, she discovered she found great solace in further developing her prayer life as she intercedes for each of them. As all parents soon realize, when their children grow up, the power to control diminishes to almost nothing—just as the children's problems mount in direct proportion. Which is why prayer becomes the weapon parents use most effectively to ward off the seen and unseen, known and unknown dangers their children face today or will face tomorrow.

As we invest daily time interceding for our adult children (with a purpose and passion known only to their parents), God honors those petitions and we find we start changing too. Circumstances that may have overwhelmed us a year ago no longer shake us; rather, we are now able to see the bigger picture where God is actively involved and working. We also find that the more swiftly we lay down our burdens at God's feet, the more quickly inner calmness replaces fear and anxiety—perhaps making much-needed room for spontaneous fun and laughter.

Take-way Action Thought

Whenever I feel overwhelmed or burdened by my children's problems, I will give thanks to you for already actively working to strengthen my children so they can endure and learn from whatever hardships they are facing.

My Heart's Cry to You, O Lord

Father, help me to see the therapeutic value of having fun with my spouse. Help me to schedule time to be alone with my spouse or even on my own—time to experience and enjoy the good things you've placed here on earth for us. I realize there will always be a multitude of problems in this life, but I never want that fact to rule me. Instead, when problems arise, give me the good sense to immediately take them to you in prayer, and then cast all my anxiety into your care and keeping. Lord, I will always be a parent with a parent's heart, but you can enable me to periodically step out of that important role to enjoy the lighter side of life, to have balance. In all things help me to live out this truth. Amen.

Chapter 19

Welcoming Untimely Interruptions

But my eyes are fixed on you, Sovereign LORD;
in you I take refuge—do not give me over to death.
Psalm 141:8

We live in the present. The past can weigh us down, but the future pulls us along. There is a destination to life. We live a story that has a past, present, and future.
Edward Welch

In everyone's life, there comes a time when something or someone introduces an untimely interruption to one's plans. Mine arrived when I least expected it, and it lingered much longer than I had hoped it would. Some ten years ago, immediately following a strain-filled several years when we lost family members, entered the caregiving role for an elderly relative, changed churches after twenty-two years, and had a house full of teenagers to raise, I had my first (of six) shoulder surgeries. Even now, I can still remember thinking to myself that it might not be the best time to undergo a major surgery. But I went ahead, ignoring that still, small voice of reason (and wisdom).

While the surgery was successful, my recovery was not. After weeks of pain-filled, sleepless nights, I fell into a depression—a real honest-to-goodness depression that left me feeling nothing at all and crying continuously. Since I'd never ever felt that way before, I was frightened that this "new me" would last forever. Thankfully, it didn't. But the road to emotional, physical, and spiritual recovery took far longer than I anticipated. It remains to me one of those life-markers you never forget, even if you wanted to.

During those long painful weeks when I had little to do but sit immobile while my shoulder healed, I had hours upon hours to reflect on my life, my beliefs, and my family (past, present, and future). It did me a world of good to stop and pay attention to what matters most in this life. What I learned the hard way was that my life (and yours) will be filled to overflowing with untimely interruptions, and we should open up our arms wide and welcome each one warmly. Why? Because each and every day of our lives is charted out by our loving heavenly Father who knows what we need most.

Untimely interruptions have been thwarting my well-laid plans for the majority of my adult life. Still, when I surrender my plans for the day to the God who supercedes everything, it's all to the good and I've found that blessings abound.

So what constitutes an untimely interruption? A phone call from your child who just wants to chat. A text announcing your son is coming home for a few days later in the week. An e-mail from a daughter who is feeling uncertain about her college major. A knock on the door (because your grandson can't reach the doorknob and turn it yet).

Truly, when we learn to discipline ourselves to see untimely interruptions as part of the ebb and flow of a full life, it's all to the good. And better yet, when we do learn to welcome these interruptions with good grace, grace abounds to us and to those who interrupt!

Untimely interruptions. Most of us hate the sound of those two words. But if you're like me, you also know that they have probably done you a lot of good over the years. How often has an interruption stopped you from doing something you realize only later that you would have regretted? How many times has an interruption stalled one plan that made way for a better idea? When have you felt stymied from accomplishing a task only to be blessed beyond measure by the interruption itself? Surprise. Surprise. God loves to surprise us, and he often uses interruptions to accomplish his desires for us.

I suspect that too often we spend much of our time busy making plans that are not part of God's overall plan for our lives. We get caught up in past regrets and spend too much effort making sure we don't make the same mistakes again, missing out on the present joys. It's true that we live lives composed of the past, present, and future, and God rules and oversees all three at the same time. God wants us to learn from our past, live in the present, and dream of the wonderful future. Imagine, then, how dull life would be if there were no surprise interruptions to our plans. As long as we know that God holds our lives in the hollow of his hands, we can confidently release our hours and days—and plans—into his hand as well. Past. Present. Future. It's all under his divine control.

Take-away Action Thought

Lord, when I begin to get frustrated by the interruptions in my day, I will stop and say a quick prayer for perception to see the possibilities from your point of view.

My Heart's Cry to You, O Lord

Father, you know how difficult I find it to get interrupted once I am busy working through my to-do list. Help me to surrender my plans to you every morning as I open my heart and mind to you in prayer. Before I even get started, remind me that you hold every hour of my day in your hands and that long ago you charted out my days, before I was even born. Help me to be flexible and not resent interruptions, no matter what form they may take. Give me your heart of service and hospitality to whoever needs it from me. And help me to remember how you have used untimely interruptions in my life to strengthen me for whatever task you've given me. Amen.

Chapter 20

Supporting Your Adult Children through a Crisis

The LORD is my shepherd, I lack nothing.
Psalm 23:1

I triumph now in thy promises as
I shall do in their performance.
Arthur Bennett

There is a biblical truth that I alternately love and hate. It's quite simple really. If I'm honest, there are days when I wish it wasn't true, but it is. Simply put, as parents, friends, family, neighbors, or colleagues, we cannot effectively bring encouragement—the powerful type that will bring rescue, hope, and change—to someone unless we've first received it from God himself for ourselves. In other words, if I haven't gone deep with God myself, and in my darkest moments discovered that his rescue, hope, and power to help change is enough, then there is no way I can pass along that confidence to another.

This principle can simultaneously comfort me and convict me. For there have been hours, days, and weeks when I felt myself completely undone and unable to bring about a "rescue mission" of sorts for myself, though I knew God could and eventually would. If in my own darkest hours I hadn't turned to him and clung tightly, I wouldn't now have a testimony of his faithfulness no matter what the need or how low I've fallen. I can speak of God's provision because: (1) his word tells me he will provide, and (2) I've experienced the validity of those promises over and over.

Which leads me to a recent event that broke my heart, my husband's heart, and my children's. When my daughter announced her pregnancy we were all excited at the possibility of welcoming grandchild number three into our family. That excitement and anticipation of first welcoming and then loving another baby cheered me up on more than one dismal day.

But when my daughter told me she had started bleeding (she had miscarried before), my heart did a sudden lurch and drop. The next ten or so weeks had all of us on our knees before the Lord, alternately asking for his healing touch or the grace to endure another day of not knowing. This wasn't a simple miscarriage (if there is such a thing). My daughter's ultrasound and blood-level readings raised some red flags that she might be experiencing a molar pregnancy (a molar pregnancy is when a noncancerous, or benign, tumor develops in the uterus—when an egg is fertilized, but the placenta develops into an abnormal mass of cysts.) If that was the case, she was in for a time of it medically.

Thus another layer of crushing grief was added to the loss of her unborn baby. As her mother, I naturally wanted to erase all the pain my daughter was enduring, but I couldn't. The best I could offer her was to love her, listen to her, pray for her, and point her back to the Great Physician, the only One who could truly and fully bring rescue, hope, and healing to her broken heart. How thankful I was that I could direct her to God, fully assured he would mend her heart—just as he'd done with me so many times before. It was a bittersweet confidence in a time of abject sorrow.

In those moments when we know we are totally helpless to change a situation, the best we can do is call to mind God's promises of provision, rescue, hope, healing—and with confidence, pass those on to our children, reminding them that God alone is qualified to enter into their suffering and help them bear it. The Lord is my shepherd (and my children's), and he has promised that when the need arises, we will lack nothing.

One of the best gifts we can pass along to our children is an unwavering confidence in God's promises to meet all our needs. As we live out this truth by example in our own lives, our children will watch how God's power and provision are displayed day by day. It's one thing to quietly believe in God's faithfulness to supply all our needs; it's quite another to speak out that confidence even before the supply has arrived.

I'm all for living a quiet life, minding my own business, and settling in the backdrop of this great big world. What I'm not for is being silent when I need to speak up or speak out. When God meets my need, I have a responsibility to share that good news with others to strengthen their faith in the same God who desires to supply their needs as well. Nothing encourages me more than hearing how God has swept in, prompted the hearts of others to offer some kind of tangible help, and used flesh-and-blood people to answer someone's desperate prayer.

We'll never quite understand how many times the Holy Spirit's nudging to act on behalf of someone else is God's plan to fulfill Psalm 23:1. But we can start praying to be more effective listeners—and then maybe we'll find out.

Take-away Action Thought

When I see my child suffering, I will pray with great expectation the tried and true promises for provision found in God's word.

My Heart's Cry to You, O Lord

How glad I am that I can call you Father. You gave me life and then gave me new birth into your family of believers. I am your child, and you have promised that I shall never lack something I need. Lord, help me to take you at your word and pray back to you your promises, believing you will answer them. My heart cries out to you as I see my children suffering and I am unable to ease their heart's pain. But you, Lord, can bring hope, healing, and a strong rescue. Give us eyes of faith to believe all that your word promises us. And give us the grace to live rejoicing in your promises, even before we witness the provision firsthand. Amen.

Chapter 21

Giving Counsel When Your Adult Children Want to Give Up

Let the morning bring me word of
your unfailing love,
for I have put my trust in you.
Show me the way I should go,
for to you I entrust my life.

Psalm 143:8

People who don't read the Bible on a daily basis must think Satan takes a day off. Good luck with that. The magnificent obsession is so foreign to my natural self that I need to be reminded of it every day. It takes me about twenty minutes to forget my highest ideals and start living selfishly again.

Gary Thomas

A friend's child became entangled in a serious, we're-heading-toward-the-altar romantic relationship with someone she shouldn't have become involved with. Everyone who loved this woman could see from the start that it wasn't going to end well. The "end" being either: (1) the mismatched couple would actually tie the knot and marry, even though their dating/courtship history was strewn with troublesome continual blowups and blow-outs; or (2) one of the pair would eventually see the light and break it off, while breaking the other's heart. Either scenario was going to be heart-wrenching and it was difficult to observe, even from a distance.

Try as my friend might to advise her daughter using biblical principles and lots of everyday life experiences and examples, her child refused to heed her mother's counsel. Two years into the off-on, up-down, roller-coaster relationship, something happened (in truth, a whole lot of "somethings" added up) that forced this young woman to face the truth. In the aftermath of her realization that this most current event was only the beginning of a life of heartaches, she finally ended the relationship.

To say this breaking-off from each other was anything less painful than entering rehab for a drug/alcohol addiction would be lying. Day after day, this young woman wept before, during, and after work. She cried with her mom. She cried with her friends. She cried herself sick. She cried herself out. Finally, she cried out to God.

As my friend tells it, watching her daughter end this relationship meant she had to rebuild her entire life structure the same way a grief-stricken widow does when her husband dies. She grieved. She raged. She wept. She denied. She finally accepted. She eventually moved on. Over time (months, not weeks or days), this young woman started to heal inside and turn significant corners in her life. She recognized that there was no one to blame but herself for what she had suffered. She also realized one of life's hardest lessons: We can make a mistake (or a whole string of them) and God forgives, he rebuilds, he restores. But there are frequently consequences resulting from our poor choices and sinful actions that don't instantly disappear once we are forgiven.

In that slow realization, this woman got firsthand experience in undoing her past and recreating her future by making wise decisions one hour at a time. Minutely slow at first, every choice she made felt foreign, felt unnatural—that is, until she started going daily to the Source of all wisdom. As she began replacing selfish choices with selfless ones, this young woman started to grow by leaps and bounds from the inside out. And those around her who have witnessed this new life rejoice with her.

The most important biblical counsel we can give or get is the call to persevere. God honors the prayers of those who keep coming to him all hours of the day or night. Consider prayer as the anytime, anywhere direct line to the only One who can offer you the hope, help, and grace you need to keep on going. And do we ever need to keep on moving forward after we've blundered badly and are bereft in our own strength to meet the challenges of life!

Parents can most encourage their children during their tough times by reminding them—and living by example—to repeatedly, persistently, and intentionally turn to God's word every single day. Only God and his word offer the supply of wise-living, we-can-endure-this, and you're-not-alone-in-your-pain type of comfort. Another important aspect of helping our children through their own personal crises is to remind them that stepping into and out of a difficult situation is never an overnight prospect. Remind them that it took some time to land where they are at now, and it's going to take some time to rebuild their life as well. If there's a final word of exhortation that our children need to hear, it's never stop persevering in persistently pursuing God. Never. Perseverance—don't make another decision without it.

Take-away Action Thought

When my children are suffering the painful consequences of their poor choices, I will push them into God's loving embrace by encouraging them to find their strength and solace in his word.

My Heart's Cry to You, O Lord

Father, today's pain doesn't surprise me. I saw it coming, and yet I couldn't stop it. You know how much my child is hurting, how sad she is over her choices. Still, she has to do an about-face and turn her broken heart and mind back toward you. As much as I would love to erase this entire situation from everyone's memory, that is impossible. So please help me stay the course and lovingly steer my child to you no matter how much time it takes. Give me—and her—the expectant hope that you can and will rebuild her life and recreate her from the inside out into the woman you know she can grow to be. Amen.

Chapter 22

Investing in People Other than Your Adult Children

Blessed is the one . . .
whose delight is in the law of the Lord,
and who meditates on his law day and night.

Psalm 1:1–2

There is more in you than what your parents, friends, teachers, fellow laborers, or leaders see in you. Don't take on limitations that don't belong to you. He is waiting and ready to give you a chance to make a difference.

John Maxwell

I remember the day I was asked to lead a women's group at my local church as if it were yesterday. Like most mothers of teens and beyond, I was looking ahead and could see that very soon all my children would either be out of the house or pretty much out, even if they still used our same home address. I pondered the request, prayed about it, and then said yes.

It didn't take me long to realize how much it benefited me to lead a group of women through one book after another.

After all, whenever you take on the responsibility of teaching on a topic or leading a discussion, you're the one who learns the most. Between the preparation time for each class and the hours I spent in prayer asking the Lord to help me lead well, I was the clear winner. Having taught my children at home during their elementary schooling years, I already knew that when you're responsible to unpack a new concept or skill, you have to know it inside out before you attempt to pass on the information to others in a way that will change their life.

What I hadn't counted on when I began leading these classes was how much I would gain personally from my interaction with other women. Sure, I have good and trusted friends with whom I'm in contact regularly and with whom I share my deepest sorrows as well as joys. But what I failed to understand was how valuable it is for women from different seasons of life to invest in one another's lives in a systemized, topic-by-topic setting.

We all seem to learn differently. We all appear to take in information and digest it in unique ways. Our perspectives and insights are ours alone until we share them. So as we met together to talk about subjects as varied as the stars in the sky, we came up with lots of interesting ways to heal hurts, overcome tragedies, and deal with ongoing heartaches. Maybe most important of all, we agreed that meeting together weekly meant we were more than simply acquaintances. We had grown into a unified body of believers who wept together and rejoiced together. The operative word here is *together*.

I've often considered how much I would have missed had I not said yes to that small request to lead a class. I wonder. What is God prompting you to do? Is he asking you to consider something new, something that may have you shaking in your boots? Or possibly, God wants you to take a break for a while and sit quietly (and alone) before him. Only you can answer the call of the Lord that he places upon your heart. Together—yes, that word again—the operative word for all growth is *together*, either with others on the same journey or for a time alone together with him.

Whenever we label ourselves as good or bad, we are limited. Truly so. I think about how many times I would tell someone who asked what I did, "I'm a mom of four children. I'm a homeschooling mother. I'm a book reviewer/columnist/author. I'm a wife. I'm a child of God." All true enough, but was it truly all?

Today, my responsibilities may limit my ability to branch out and try something new and maybe a little scary. Tomorrow, though, everything may look different. Let's not say no in our minds before we've given God the chance to tell us yes. Let's not limit what he may ask us to do before he even has had time to work through all the ifs/ands/or buts in our hearts.

Parents, I fear, frequently define themselves by their parenthood alone, which is fine while they are primarily parenting. But once the children exit the home, these same people who've honed a variety of skills over the years are now much freer to say yes—a resounding yes!—the next time opportunity knocks. Let's all declare before the Lord that we will not limit his plans and purposes for our lives. *Together* we can make a difference.

Take-away Action Thought

The next time someone asks me to take on a new project or fill a role, I will refuse to say no until I have prayed it through.

My Heart's Cry to You, O Lord

Lord, will you help me to keep and maintain an open mind? All too often, I get stuck in the mind-set that my life is already too full, because for many years that was the truth while I was parenting day and night. But now, my life is different. I have more time. Help me to remember that I also have more skills and abilities than at any other season in my life. God, help me to look for ways to get involved with others outside of my four walls and to do so with a humble yet positively expectant spirit. I truly believe you have wonderful plans for my life, and I don't want to miss one of them. Amen.

Chapter 23

Allowing Adult Children to Move Back Home

Search me, O God, and know my heart;
test me and know my anxious thoughts.
Psalm 139:23

A new idea is delicate. It can be killed by a sneer or a yawn; it can be stabbed to death by a joke or worried to death by a frown on the right person's brow.
Charles Brower

It's always wonderful, and often insightful, to have at least a few friends who are farther along in life than you are because: (1) they can offer excellent tried and true methods of handling life's tough times; and (2) you can see up close how each stage of life brings with it some beautiful gifts. Enter my good friend from across the country who has two adult children and three grandchildren. She was just getting her feet wet as a women's speaker and succeeding marvelously when her unmarried daughter, a young adult career woman, told her she was pregnant. My friend and her husband were saddened that their daughter wasn't planning on marrying the father of her child, but they supported their daughter and tried to help her prepare for her upcoming delivery.

Soon after the birth of their granddaughter, my friend's daughter announced she was moving out of the apartment she had shared with her boyfriend and asked if she could move back home until she completed her college degree. My friend and her spouse spent much time discussing and praying about this huge life change because they knew—better than their daughter did—how much adjusting would have to happen for them to live together under the same roof as adults. Peaceably, that is.

So my friend and her husband drew up a contract of sorts to keep the peace. At first, their daughter wondered if they really were okay with her moving in with a new baby in tow. They were, but it was because they wanted to create a loving environment for their daughter and granddaughter that my friend looked ahead and anticipated all possible points of contention that could arise when an adult child moves back home. Sure, there were some snags they had to get through from time to time. And it was most certainly an adjustment for my friend and her spouse to go from an empty nest to having a daughter and a newborn in their home 24/7. But it worked.

Periodically, I've asked my friend how it's working out since her daughter has been "home" for over a year now. Her honesty is another reason why I love and admire her. Overall, the living situation is good, but there are moments when she longs for solitude and silence (and you don't get much of either with a growing baby). However, my friend also realizes that this arrangement is just for a season. It will pass and before she knows it, her daughter will have completed her degree and found work that will support her and her daughter. So instead of bemoaning some lost privileges of being an empty-nester, my friend focuses on the positive and keeps on moving forward.

What have I learned from her? That life is always changing, and in spite of how we might envision our future, it can change in an instant. So, just as my friend does, I choose to hold tightly to the Lord and lightly to my life as I have pictured it.

Since life is always changing, moving forward, and never at a standstill, it's important for us to hold tight to God because the ride will get bumpy before it's over. It's also essential to look for the positive in the midst of change. I don't know anyone who wouldn't feel a little upended once all their children had moved out, only to have one (or more) move back home.

How else can we assist others who are facing a situation as my friend did? Affirm them and applaud them for their kindness and generosity. Make sure you spend time building them up emotionally and spiritually, because they're going to need that encouragement on days when their house feels just a little too cramped and a lot too noisy. Help your friend see the beauty of being there as a bridge between jobs, educational goals, moves across the country, or—more difficult—those involving relational breakups and breakdowns. The truth is that it's always a blessing to serve.

Do more than simply nod your head when your friend shares her worries and concerns; help her devise a practical plan for making it work out. Then offer to pitch in and help rearrange furniture, buy needed household goods, and just be there with a hopeful, positive attitude. Day in and day out, remind your friend that what she is doing matters.

Take-away Action Thought

When I feel some task or service is too much to take on, Lord, help me to see the beauty of serving others—which means including my family in that vision.

My Heart's Cry to You, O Lord

Lord, I know you fully understand how I'm feeling when all my plans for my hours/days, as well as my house, are being upended. I want to offer our home to our children when they are in need. I want them always to feel secure in the knowledge that they have a place here with us should the need arise. I know myself well, however, and I have become used to alone time, quietness, tidiness even, which will take some adjusting on my part to overcome. Help me to be a generous and gracious parent by opening not just the door to my home, but my heart as well. Give me the eternal perspective that investing in people is always the highest calling. Amen.

Chapter 24

Banishing Worry for Good

How abundant are the good things
that you have stored up for those who fear you.
Psalm 31:19

My advice to you is not to inquire why or whither, but just enjoy the ice cream while it's on your plate.
Thornton Wilder

Thirty years ago my husband and I were invited to dinner. After we had enjoyed that lovely meal with good friends who were older and wiser than us, I sat my very pregnant self onto their comfy couch and felt my firstborn kick. As I contemplated motherhood, I simultaneously began worrying about whether or not my soon-to-graduate-from-college spouse would get a teaching job immediately after graduation. The truth was that we didn't intend for me to get pregnant so soon after our marriage. Being the planners that both of us are, we figured around the three-year mark would be a great time to start thinking about babies (bearing them and rearing them).

But God. How many times in my life have I made detailed plans, set elaborate goals, and put pen to paper, only to have God totally disregard every single idea I had formulated? If I had to venture a guess, I would say many more times than seeing my plans fulfilled. *But God.* Now, I can look back and laugh at how simple I was in my thinking. I honestly wouldn't have said I was trying to control my destiny. Rather, I earnestly believed we should be good stewards of everything given us, including the preparation for a family.

But God. As I sat worrying that evening long ago, a strange look must have passed across my face because one of our friends asked me what was wrong. I went on to tell him that I was afraid my husband wouldn't have a job by the time our baby arrived. He listened to me talk and worry, and worry and talk. Then he asked me if worry ever did me any good. I stopped. Now that you mention it, worry hadn't done one thing to help me figure out a problem, devise a solution, or rest easy at night.

Our friend then challenged me in the kindest way by sharing Bible verses with me on handling fear with trust in God. He told me there were 365 verses in the Bible that dealt with fear/worry—one for every day of the year. Next, he asked me some more introspective questions that got me thinking hard about how much I *said* I trusted God in all things—as opposed to how much I really *did* trust him for real life problems.

But God. Since that conversation over three decades ago, I've remembered that challenge to trust God frequently in times of great struggle, often in relation to my children, when I wasn't sure I could get through a trying time. Little did I realize back then on that night, even before I became a mother, that the challenge to trust God for all things, at all times, in all ways, was only the beginning of a lifetime of placing my will on the altar before him. Learning to relinquish my control, or more accurately the illusion of control, was one of the most important lessons ever.

But God. It means knowing in the deepest part of my heart and soul that God is going to take care of me and mine, and that he has stored up goodness for me and mine. It also means that I lay down the burden of worry day by day and truly be present in the moment, relishing whatever it is I'm experiencing right now. *But God*. Enough said.

Letting go of control is a beautiful thing. It's freeing to know—really know—in the depths of your being that God has your back. That God has stored up and planned good things for you and those you love. That God loves us so much, he wants us to live in this moment of time. Because of this simple two-word phrase, *But God*, we can be there. Be all there. In every moment of time, fully relishing life in its infinite beauty and variety.

Worrying now or later will starve the joy out of our lives faster than anything. It holds us captive in its grip. Worry ruins even the most perfect moment by staining it with its sin. Yes, worry is sin. God commands us to trust him in all things, at all times. When we opt to take back the reins of our life and worry over the large and the small, we sin.

Instead of worrying our way through life, let's start saying out loud, *But God*. This mighty statement reminds us, and everyone within earshot, that we know our God's faithfulness. That we trust in his power and might to take care of us. That we are sure and certain he has good planned for us. *But God*. I just love the sound of it. Do you?

Take-away Action Thought

When I am tempted to worry, I will speak the words "But God" out loud.

My Heart's Cry to You, O Lord

Father, you know how easy it is for me to go down the path of worry. It doesn't take much of a bump in the road to rattle me. To my shame, I can all too quickly grab the steering wheel back from you and try to make things right, without even asking you to intervene. Help me, Lord, to stop myself before I travel down the path of worry and end up fretting, fuming, and frustrated. Teach me to turn quickly to you at all times. During the good times and the bad times, you are always my righteous ruler and desire the very best for me. Enable me to live in the "right now." To be here. To not forfeit this moment's joy in sinful worry. Amen.

Chapter 25

Applying Tough Love as Needed

In peace I will lie down and sleep,
for you alone, LORD,
make me dwell in safety.
Psalm 4:8

Our openness, when fitting, makes us a magnet for the people around us who are longing for just one person in their lives to be "real," to listen to their story without raising an eyebrow, to let them weep without providing advice.
Carol Kent

It wasn't the first time I had felt that inner nudge to share some of the painful details of when my daughter was running wild, driving us crazy with worry and fear. There I sat, at the head of a large table surrounded by my peers, when one woman remarked, "You're so blessed to have children who love the Lord and are serving him." She went to tell us about her drug-addicted son, who was the love of her life and yet simultaneously causing her untold heartache and grief. I could have just nodded my head and redirected the conversation, but that would have been wrong and selfish of me.

So I shared that most difficult time of my life (thus far). As always when I retell that story, I tend to get emotional and my voice catches as I explain to others (and to this hurting mother in particular) that all was not so rosy in our family. I explained about my daughter's dangerous choices, her drinking, partying, and hanging out with risky young men who wouldn't have cared less if she ended up dead in a ditch or at the back of an alley. Even though I don't like dredging up these memories, because they still hurt to talk about, I realize that it's because of my daughter's self-willed journey into darkness and then into the light that she is able to testify to God's faithfulness today. And testify she does.

However, part of what I share with other hurting parents is the time when a police officer knocked on our door after we had reported her missing. I was obviously distraught in the extreme, and I'll never forget what this wise young policeman said to me: "I see this all the time—parents who are trying to get their children back on track but the children don't want any part of it. So the parents pay for their children's mistakes and it breaks their hearts." Then he looked straight at me and said, "We'll find your daughter, but once we get her back home, you don't have to allow her to live here anymore." Slam! Who knew how directly that single sentence would hit me?

Somehow, in the midst of our fear and sorrow, this officer of the law reminded us that our daughter, now an adult, didn't have to live inside our home. It was our choice.

Once we were reunited with her, my husband and I created a house-rule list that she had to sign and abide by or she would be given two weeks to find another place to live. I'm sure there were multiple influencing factors at work in her heart during that time, but it was at this juncture that she realized her friends weren't friends at all—and that if we kicked her out, she would have nowhere to go. That day her life began to change. Inch by inch. Small choices here and there. Lots of tears, some of anger, some of regret. But she started to walk in a different direction.

Years later, we talked about what made the difference in her choosing to continue to walk on the wild side or heed our counsel. She said she finally realized we loved her unconditionally and her friends didn't. Over time—after much love, counseling, and enduring some tough discipline—she told me she never wanted to go back to that empty life. I'm so thankful that the policeman God sent to our home that day encouraged us to step up and create firm boundaries for our daughter. Tough love can make all the difference.

One of the areas that suffers the most for parents when children are in trouble is sleep. We worry, we fret, and we toss and turn all through the night. I've been challenged more times than I can count by good friends who remind me that I don't need to worry about anything—God stays awake all night long handling the big and the small, allowing me to rest in safety. I'm all for a good night's sleep, and a nap during the day as required, because parenting during those especially tough times exhausts us in every way possible.

After all, how can we give wise counsel to our children when we can't think straight? How can we exercise the self-control required during those challenging seasons when we're so beat that our nerves are taut? We can't, which is why we need to meditate upon and memorize Psalm 4:8: "In peace I will lie down and sleep, for you alone, Lord, make me dwell in safety." I need to know that God is sovereign (the Bible tells me so), and I need to rest easy knowing he is watching over me and those I love (the Bible tells me so).

Rest—the real down-to-earth, deep-in-your-bones rest—is what every parent needs when their children's choices stretch them to the limit through the waking hours. As impossible as it seems, I know for sure (because I've experienced it) that God can and will give us sleep in the night when we ask for it and trust him to bring it about. Ask. Trust. Rest.

Take-away Action Thought

When my children's choices are harming them and us, I will not shy away from putting into place tough love, because I want to love them for the long run.

My Heart's Cry to You, O Lord

Father, just as you sometimes use tough love to get and keep our attention, give us the wisdom and strength to enact that kind of long-lasting love with our children. We recognize that there are times when a simple conversation is not enough, and we are forced to set up rules that unless followed will result in some tough consequences. It is difficult to put this type of discipline into place, but we do so because we love our children so very much. Help us to stay strong, to not give way, and to pray, pray, pray until our children have turned back to you. Amen.

Chapter 26

Being Hopeful When Your Adult Child's Life Falls Apart

"In your distress you called and I rescued you,
I answered you out of a thundercloud."
Psalm 81:7

Courage is fear that has said its prayers.
Karle Wilson Baker

Although I do not much like the daily aches and pains of growing older, I am in full-speed ahead mode when it comes to gaining a more even-keeled, even-tempered perspective on problems. The longer we live, the more perspective-minded we should be. As a rule, I can hear some pretty devastating news without it bringing me to my knees. This is good.

It's not that I'm heartless or have grown cold toward the hurts of others. Rather, in my best friend's words, I now realize that I have only a certain amount in my emotional bank account, and I don't want to squander that energy on issues I can't change. My friend and I often confer on the daily ups/downs of midlife with aging parents, grown-up children, and now grandchildren. It's like we're smack-dab in the middle of three generations, each with their own special needs and challenges, and some days we have only a few cents left in our emotional bank account. Other days, we're in the red.

Which is why when one of my children comes to me discouraged or fearful of a choice their sibling (or child) has made, I don't always immediately react as they might think I should. Two reasons being: (1) I'm a whole lot older and have been through these tough seasons with more people than I can count (or remember), thus I have some perspective that all may not be as bad as it first appears; and (2) God has strengthened me and my faith to see past today's struggles (or someone's poor decisions), because I've seen God bring people back to himself more times than I can count (or remember). This is good.

I've learned the hard way that I can walk through the valley, worrying day and night about my child, or I can say my prayers and trust God to answer me out of my own personal thundercloud of despair. Having done both at different junctures of life, I can honestly speak to the wisdom of gaining real courage to face whatever comes when I take my rightful place at God's footstool and humble myself before his presence, pleading for his help. It's true: "Courage is fear that has said its prayers." Have you said yours today?

Though I briefly addressed the issue of our emotional bank accounts, I'd like to comment further on this important principle. As people age, they usually see their limits in obvious ways physically, and they understand these limits in strength and endurance, making adjustments in their lifestyle to accommodate these changes. Few folks realize, however, that they might also have limitations to their emotional energy reserve, which is why some fall into depression during those periods of greatest stress. I remember my husband telling me that it was good for me to care deeply about the needs of others, but I wasn't built (nor is anyone) to take on everyone's burdens and carry them day in and day out. Certainly, we are to help ease the loads of those we come into contact with—but some people do it to the extreme, and then their health (emotional and otherwise) is stripped from them.

Therein lies the beauty of this principle of mentally weighing a problem and deciding if you can spare the emotional energy required to handle it. This doesn't mean you stop caring. It does mean that the information about the problem won't drive you to tears and distraction. We can live our lives with a great deal more emotional equilibrium if we remember to (1) place every problem into the light of eternity with its limitless perspective, and (2) call to mind that God has always been, and always will be, faithful to work things through. This is good.

Take-away Action Thought

When the next piece of bad news comes to me, I will ask God to give me his eternal perspective and remind me of his enduring faithfulness.

My Heart's Cry to You, O Lord

Lord, today I'm on the receiving end of news that does indeed cause my heart to skip a beat. I'm concerned, I care, and I so want to jump into the situation and try to make it right. But you and I, Lord, both know that all people have their own spiritual journeys to walk, and I cannot short-circuit another's path just because I think I know better. Help me to remember your great faithfulness in all the times past when I've cried out to you. Help me to maintain an eternal perspective that realizes anything can, and often does, change from one day to the next. This is good. Amen.

Chapter 27

Praying for Something You Can't Talk About

Answer me when I call to you,
  my righteous God.
Give me relief from my distress;
  be merciful to me and hear my prayer.

Psalm 4:1

Our Father will refresh us with many pleasant inns on the journey, but he would not encourage us to mistake them for home.

C. S. Lewis

There are those infuriatingly painful events that morph into hours and then days, weeks, months—years even—when something happens to someone you love and you are powerless to prevent, halt, or even ease the sorrow. Every parent has known this desperate place when no matter what you are doing or where you are heading, your thoughts attach themselves to "the problem" just like superglue. We pray. We worry-pray. We cry out to God for mercy. We beg a little or a lot. We worry-pray some more. Still, there is silence. Often there is no resolution.

Just more internal combustion with no release until finally we are left speechless, bewildered, and spent—and often right where God wants us.

At the time of this writing, I'm sitting at the tail end of a long season of having to watch one of my children suffer. To say that I've been able to "keep calm and keep on keeping on" through the last six months would be a lie. Even this morning as I sat contemplating a particular promise in Scripture, I realized how much I have failed to stay strong in my own faith during my child's time of testing.

I recognized by the ongoing agitation in my heart, and by the grace of God, that I didn't much like my own reactions these past weeks and months. Truth told, I'd become in part the very type of individual who had been inflicting pain upon my child. Ouch. Confessions aside, I realized I had my own weighty sins to deal with in addition to working to forgive someone else. How did I end up so entangled emotionally and anxiety-ridden? It was pretty easy: I just couldn't accept what God was allowing, and I didn't want to relinquish my child to his care.

In the midst of my child's season of suffering (and mine by association), I've learned a few things. In my darkest feeling-like-my-hands-are-tied moments, I recognized how little control I have over the events in my young, adult children's lives. Although I would have given lip service to this truth all along, now I feel it with every breath I take. Little kids equal little problems. Big kids equal adult-sized problems.

Still, God has slowly but surely released my vise-like grip over my child's situation to allow him to help me surrender my child's future and well-being into his capable care. Merciful as he is, whenever I thought I would go crazy if this situation persisted another day, he surprised me with reminders of his love and faithfulness—just enough to get my attention, just enough to give me hope, just enough to remind me that he still ruled over all, quieting my fears and silencing the voices in my head. And it's funny, but looking back at what God did for me, I see it was enough. Just enough. It always is.

Let's be clear: there will be times in each of our lives when no one but the Lord can fully understand the painful burdens we bear. Spouses, friends, family may all make the attempt to enter into our heart's pain because they care for us, but there are moments when God alone is strong enough to bear our heart's cries. Words, anyone's words, just won't cut it. In the same way that others cannot ease our heart's pain, we have to recognize God wants us parents to take our children's burdens to him as well.

It is a wonderful thing to come alongside our child who is struggling with doubt, discouragement, depression, and despair. But isn't there an even more powerful call to pray? I wonder how often I've muddied the waters with my words or my actions. Well-intentioned though they are, God wants me to take my burdens to him in prayer and allow him to work behind the scenes, within my children's hearts, and bring restoration in a way that only he can accomplish.

Parenting adult children means checking ourselves at every turn and asking what God expects of us now that they are grown. We can't run interference in the same way we did when they were in elementary, middle, or high school. What we can do is turn our frets, fears, and worry-prayers into constant intercession with the glad expectation that God both hears and answers our cries. I know that every difficult encounter I experience reminds me that this world is not my home. It never has been and it never will be—that truth shores up my heart. So why wouldn't God want my children to grasp this wonderful promise by allowing them to experience life's hardships? After all, like me, my children were made for another world too.

Take-away Action Thought

When I see this broken world harming my children, let my immediate response be to pray.

My Heart's Cry to You, O Lord

Father, thank you for reminding me through the promises I read in your word that you truly do rule over all creation. I take great comfort in knowing that you see every event that happens in my life and in the lives of those I love. When I cannot offer comfort, when I am restrained from easing pain inflicted on my children, help me to take those concerns directly to you. Lord, although you've given me a parent's heart, never let me forget that you love my children more than I do and that you alone know how to love them best. Amen.

Chapter 28

Asking for Forgiveness as Needed

But with you there is forgiveness.
Psalm 130:4

Wisdom is found along a path that is strewn with our own sets of fears and insecurities to be faced. We must do the thing we think we cannot do. It's in the doing that the strength comes.
Paula Rinehart

We were standing side by side—shoveling flavored popcorn into paper bags in anticipation of a couple hundred sticky hands who would be reaching for this tasty treat—when my friend told me about her letter. My dear friend has been through a lot in her life. Some of the pain she has endured has come from the hands of others. Some, she'll tell you, arrived by her own poor choices born of a heart that had been broken one too many times.

Regardless of my friend's painful past, she is the mother of two young men. Both of her sons are smart, accomplished, and good at whatever they turn their time and attention toward accomplishing. Both endured their parents' difficult divorce, spending time with their mom and their dad alternately over the years. But that is where the similarities stop.

One son, a man of faith and of grace, loves and respects his mom, and you'd never know they had some difficult years as mother and son. His brother, a man who has rejected the God who loves him and the mother who has asked for his forgiveness for failing him so many years ago, is hell-bent on making my friend pay for her past mistakes. Two sons—two completely different responses to a call for forgiveness. It breaks my heart every time I think about it, so I pray.

My friend has been trying to reach out over the past few years to her estranged adult son through letters, cards, phone calls, and texts—trying and trying and trying some more to demonstrate to him that she is a different person now. Because she is different. From her breaking and burdened heart, she tells me she continues to pray for her son every day. She won't ever give up praying for him, loving him, and hoping that God will reach into his heart of pain (for which she is partly responsible) and bring the same hope and healing my friend now experiences.

And yet my friend's experience reminds me that we can go to someone we've hurt and ask for forgiveness, but they alone are responsible for their choice to forgive or not. Even though my friend's son has chosen to harden his heart against her, she is free from the inside out because she has pursued peace at the great cost of personal rejection. He has spurned her love time and time again. But as my friend told me about her most recent attempt to reach out through a letter, I could see that she was at peace. Hurting? Yes, it always hurts when we are rejected. But my friend's face told a bigger story—Jesus is her peace, no matter what circumstances might otherwise suggest.

We've all felt that ongoing sense of unease when God nudges us to make something right out of something gone wrong. It doesn't matter if it's a conflict with our spouse, friend, colleague, or neighbor, God's Spirit is relentless until we obey. Wouldn't it be a perfect world if once we saw our wrong and admitted this to the person we hurt, they would throw their arms around us in gratitude and glee? Real life isn't nearly so neat and tidy.

The beauty of asking for forgiveness is that God's grace, power, and provision go right along with us as we seek pardon for what we've done. No matter how big or small, we can rest assured that God forgives our sins and wipes them from his memory. In the safety of that response from our Savior, we can go in confidence that as we ask for forgiveness from others (especially our children), God's Spirit leads the way. Our obedience pleases him.

If we are granted the good gift of forgiveness, then praise the Lord. If we are not, then praise the Lord anyway and keep praying for it until forgiveness does come. Just as my friend is committed to seeing forgiveness come to her and her son, let us pray, pray, and pray some more whenever hardened hearts and minds confront us. Let us bring our petitions to the throne of grace, knowing he hears us and will supply us with the humility to make things right where they've gone wrong.

Take-away Action Thought

Give me ears to hear when you prompt me to ask for forgiveness. Then give me the courage to pursue peace with those I've offended.

My Heart's Cry to You, O Lord

Lord, you and I both know how I've failed to be the parent I had hoped to be when I was younger. You've shown me how my poor choices have hurt my children over the years. Words can't express how broken I feel and how disappointed I am in myself. Give me the courage and the grace to ask for forgiveness from my beloved children. Open their hearts and minds to see that I am sincere and only want to make up for my failings. Give me another chance, Lord, and guide me as I seek restoration with my family. Amen.

Chapter 29

Learning from Your Adult Children with Grace

My thoughts trouble me and I am distraught.
Psalm 55:2

You will certainly carry out God's purpose, however you act, but it makes a difference to you whether you serve like Judas or like John.
C. S. Lewis

Parenting is a funny thing—funny, as in both peculiar and comical, depending on which end of the spectrum you're standing in at the present moment. When parents are young(er) and the children are small(er), we are necessarily doing the bulk of the teaching—otherwise known as the endless instruction stage. Endless. Instruction. It seems that the role of parental endless instructor/coach/tutor/cheerleader/example leader stage will never change. Then it does.

Children get a little older and the former endless instructor role slowly begins to unravel until the majority of it lies discarded in messy heaps around the parent's feet, creating tiny little ribbons of memories. Most parents don't mind this shift because some other mighty powerful and positive changes take its place.

Endless instructor gives way to a less definable parental role. As the children grow into teens, then young adults, then young adults who move out, find gainful employment, marry, and have children, the former endless instructor parent releases a sigh of grateful relief. Even those parents who know full well that they made plenty of mistakes during their endless instructor stage of parenting emit a happy sigh because from all outward appearances all appears to be ending well. Until it doesn't.

Endless instructor (also known as parent on patrol and in control) gradually morphs into no-control, out-of-control, what-can-my-child-be-thinking parent. I've seen it happen over and over and over. Parents who have just handed the reins to their adult children (and done so with grace and class) suddenly turn back on their decisions (and on their children) when they realize their adult children are living out their lives on their terms and not living out their parents' dreams and desires for them.

I'm not talking about adult children suddenly going wild. Rather, bucking against our adult children when they make life decisions we never expected them to make because we had pretty much predicted how their lives would play out. Safe? Comfortable? Secure? What comes as a shock to so many parents is that they raised their children to be independent, smart, critical thinkers who are capable to making wise choices on their own, but those choices may differ from those their folks would make.

Time and again, I've sat with a crying mother who was wringing her hands (and heart) over some decision her adult child made that left her distraught. It could be that your child is obeying the gentle nudge from the Holy Spirit to train as a missionary to a developing country. Perhaps your son has decided he wants to join the Air Force and serve on the front lines. Or maybe your daughter has decided she's called to a life of singleness to serve the Lord, thus no grandchildren for you. Whatever our adult children do with their lives, isn't it of primary importance that we applaud them for listening to God's call for them? Isn't that the highest purpose of all? Yes, indeed. Sometimes, in ways we least expect, every one of us parents will learn something from our children if we're paying attention to what matters most. And in those turnabout moments when the parent instructor becomes the child learner, we could benefit from a gentle knowing hug and a kiss on the cheek to make "it" all better.

Who doesn't value a teachable moment, an attentive listener, a spirit of the heart characterized by humility? We are all grateful for such gifts when we take the time to carefully present a new topic, teach on a favorite subject, share a bit good news, or simply open our hearts and communicate what we dream of accomplishing someday.

However much we say we appreciate such principled qualities in others (especially when we've worked hard to develop them in our children's lives), we as parents of adult children sometimes fail to reciprocate these godly traits toward them when they come to us with their ideas, plans, and decisions.

For sure, there will be times when our children make unwise choices, and it is our duty (and privilege) to gently redirect them. Still, if our adult children make their decisions in the right way, for the right reasons, we dare not stand in their way because we had something different in mind for them. As they grow up, and we slowly step out of the endless instructor role, let's step back and give our children the room they need to make their decisions. Moreover, let's purpose to genuinely adopt a teachable spirit when they next come to share their plans with their hearts in their hands.

Take-away Action Thought

If my children make choices that upset my long-anticipated or hoped-for plans for them, I will, by your grace, never stand in their way of obeying your call on their lives by discouraging them.

My Heart's Cry to You, O Lord

Lord, I know that since my children have been young, I've privately nurtured certain dreams and desires for each of their futures. I have spent untold hours teaching them to live their lives in a way that brings you honor. I have worn out the knees on my pants by praying and praying for their well-being. Help me now to graciously step back and trust that you will guide their paths. I know that you hear my cries and that you know I truly want the best for my children. You also know that I often don't understand what that best will look like, so give me your grace and peace to keep me from fearing the unknown. Teach me, Lord, how to rightly parent my children now that they are adults capable of making their own decisions. Amen.

Chapter 30

Loving Them Unconditionally

I have hidden your word in my heart
that I might not sin against you.
Psalm 119:11

Talk is not cheap because interpretation is not cheap. The way we interpret life determines how we will respond to it.
Paul Tripp

A sudden hush swept around the room as this worn-to-the-bone mother of a wayward son uttered the words we had been expecting. She spoke with little emotion. She didn't need to raise her voice or punctuate her words in the slightest, because what she said said it all: "I don't like my son. In fact, I haven't liked him for years now. But I still love him."

Is it possible to love someone but not like them? That depends on whom you're listening to. Popular culture will say that you have to like someone first, then comes love. God's word says otherwise. We love someone whether we like them or not. Love as described in 1 Corinthians 13 gives us the proper definition of unconditional love, and it has nothing to do with "liking" or not "liking" someone. It has, however, everything to do with how we choose to act and speak.

In fact, as my friend so aptly spoke, you can certainly love your child without liking who they become, how they act, or how they choose to live their life. While some might argue that we're talking about a mere interpretation of words, we aren't. Loving a child you don't necessarily like continues to remain a point of obedience to the God we love and serve. The truth is that we're called to overcome evil with good, to pray for those who spitefully use us, and to bless our enemies and meet their needs if possible.

So when my friend dared to speak the words aloud that she does indeed love her son while not liking him, her honesty challenged me. It also provoked me to take an introspective look into my own heart and how I use my words when my adult children say or do something that displeases me. As this mother shared her heart's struggle to find ways to connect to her son in his adult years, she admitted that she found it difficult to speak in ways that communicated love, kindness, gentleness, and compassion, because in her heart of hearts, she was raging against his lifestyle. It is the heart that needs attending to before the words will flow naturally in love.

Her honesty begs the question to all of us who want to honor God with our words and build bridges through communication to our children, even when we may go through seasons when we honestly don't like them or what they are doing. As my friend revealed the depth of her struggle with using her words in a godly way, we all felt compassion for her. We likewise experienced a jolt of sad reality when it hit us, because we all had to admit how often we've fallen short in this area. It's never a simple thing to love your child when you don't like them. But God's word tells us to do so regardless. The first step to that obedience starts within our hearts and then the loving words will flow.

In a broken world such as ours, learning to apply the biblical principle of "overcoming evil with good" is essential, not optional. It's especially challenging when we find ourselves with the heartbreaking discovery that we don't much like our child at that given moment of time—which is why we make wise plans before the next conversation even starts. Sound absurd? Think of it this way: we spend hours, weeks even, planning a vacation or a holiday gathering. We envision how perfectly every detail we plan will fall into place. We see it even, in our mind's eye. Yet how often do we ever plan how to converse biblically with someone we say we love but may not like? Rarely? Ever? Never?

The hard truth is that some of our most trying conversations will take place with those who are closest to us—family. Even during the best of times, and with those with whom we have little or no conflict, how we choose to speak matters. It matters, as author Paul Tripp so eloquently states, because words are interpreted to mean something important. How we choose to converse will either draw someone closer to us (and to eventual peace) or will push them farther away (to a permanent standoff).

As a good friend once reminded me, "You can be right or you can have a relationship with your child." For me, I'd much prefer the relationship. And the relationship will come about only when I choose carefully how to use my words in a way that demonstrates unconditional love. How about you? How much are you willing to pay to be "right"?

Take-away Action Thought

When I anticipate a possible difficult conversation, I will spend time rehearsing what I will say and how I will say it—and pray, pray, pray.

My Heart's Cry to You, O Lord

Lord, as difficult as it is to admit, there are moments when I honestly do not like my child. I confess to harboring feelings of anger and resentment toward him. Help me to temper my words and hold them in check. Give me the wisdom and the inner peace to quietly spend time in your presence, reflecting upon how I might bring about a peaceful and God-honoring resolution to those moments of conflict. Help me to remove myself from the situation and step back so I might see more clearly and hear from you more directly. I want to enjoy a close and loving relationship with my child, and I know this is only possible if we learn how to converse kindly and respectfully with each other. Give me the grace to love him with every word I speak. Unconditionally. Amen.

Sources for Quotations

1. Paula Rinehart, *Strong Women, Soft Hearts* (Nashville, TN: Thomas Nelson, 2001), 84.
2. Randy Alcorn, *90 Days of God's Goodness* (Colorado Springs, CO: Multnomah, 2011), 225.
3. Anonymous (online quote).
4. Max Lucado, *Before Amen* (Nashville, TN: Thomas Nelson, 2014), 44.
5. Debbie Macomber, *One Perfect Word* (New York: Howard Books, 2012), 167.
6. Edward Welch, *Running Scared* (Greensboro, SC: New Growth Press, 2007), 41.
7. Samuel Smiles, *Life's Little Rule Book* (Lancaster, PA: Starburst, 1999), 81.
8. Anonymous, *Life's Little Rule Book* (Lancaster, PA: Starburst, 1999), 13.
9. Gary Thomas, *A Lifelong Love* (Colorado Springs, CO: David C. Cook, 2014), 142.
10. John Wilmont, *Life's Little Rule Book* (Lancaster, PA: Starburst, 1999), 35.
11. Paul Tripp, *Age of Opportunity* (Philipsburg, NJ: P & R Publishing, 2001), 36.

12. Charles Stanley, *Every Day in His Presence* (Nashville, TN: Thomas Nelson, 2014), 340.
13. Nancy Leigh DeMoss, *Choosing Gratitude* (Chicago, IL: Moody Publishers, 2009).
14. Max Lucado, *Everyday Blessings* (Nashville, TN: Thomas Nelson, 2004), 328.
15. Benjamin Franklin (online quote).
16. Helen Keller, *Life's Little Rule Book* (Lancaster, PA: Starburst, 1999), 73.
17. Bo Stern, *When Holidays Hurt* (Nashville, TN: Thomas Nelson, 2014), 61.
18. Nancy Leigh DeMoss, *Choosing Gratitude* (Chicago, IL: Moody Publishers, 2009), 103.
19. Edward Welch, *Depression: A Stubborn Darkness* (Winston-Salem, NC: Punch Press, 2004), 166.
20. Arthur Bennett, *The Valley of Vision* (Carlisle, PA: The Banner of Truth Trust, 2007), 49.
21. Gary Thomas, *A Lifelong Love* (Colorado Springs, CO: David C. Cook, 2014), 135.
22. John Maxwell, *Learning from the Giants* (Nashville, TN: FaithWords, 2014), 72.
23. Charles Brower, *Life's Little Rule Book* (Lancaster, PA: Starburst, 1999), 9.
24. Thornton Wilder, *Life's Little Rule Book* (Lancaster, PA: Starburst, 1999), 24.
25. Carol Kent, *A New Kind of Normal* (Nashville, TN: Thomas Nelson, 2007), 115.
26. Karle Wilson Baker, *Life's Little Rule Book* (Lancaster, PA: Starburst, 1999), 45.

27. C. S. Lewis (online quote).

28. Paula Rinehart, *Strong Women, Soft Hearts* (Nashville, TN: Thomas Nelson, 2001), 168.

29. C. S. Lewis, *The Problem of Pain* (New York: Harper Collins, 2002), 616.

30. Paul Tripp, *War of Words* (Philipsburg, NJ: P & R Publishing, 2000), 15.